# THE FOUNTAINWELL DRAMA TEXTS

# BEN JONSON

# THE ALCHEMIST

Edited by
S. MUSGROVE

OLIVER & BOYD
EDINBURGH

OLIVER AND BOYD
Croythorn House
23 Ravelstan Terrace
Edinburgh EH4 3TJ
(A Division of Longman Group Ltd.)

First Published 1968
Reprinted 1972, 1976

Paperback   05 001685 7

Printed in Hong Kong by
Yu Luen Offset Printing Factory Ltd.,

# ACKNOWLEDGMENTS

Every editor of Jonson must base his work on the great Oxford edition by C. H. Herford and Percy and Evelyn Simpson. This edition, like all others, gleans after them. They are referred to throughout as " *H.S.*"

I should also like to thank Dr A. J. Gurr, of Leeds University, and Mr Brian W. M. Scobie, of Oliver and Boyd, for their untiring patience and generous assistance.

S. M.

*Auckland*
*1967*

# CONTENTS

# CRITICAL INTRODUCTION

Jonson, born about 1572, was a Londoner, educated at Westminster school under Camden. He worked for his stepfather, a builder, fought as a soldier in Flanders, married, and was a professional actor by 1597. He revealed little of his intimate beliefs—we do not know, for example, why he joined, and then left, the Catholic Church; but the burly extrovert figure of legend must have been moved by "a subjectivity as intense as Donne's masquerading as its opposite".[1]

He made his name in 1598 with *Every Man in His Humour*. Jonson's prime service to Elizabethan comedy was to give it structure and coherence, firm plotting and clear characterisation. The overshadowing genius of Shakespeare tends to hide its need of such reform. For his models he went to the best source, the classics, and *The Alchemist* observes strictly the prescribed unities of time, place, and action; but his work is not "classical" in any sense that separates it from his contemporaries. Like any informed person of his time, he saw the purpose of comedy as sanative—to expose, and purge by laughter, the monstrous follies and vices of men; but, like Pope, he held this critical position because of a personal sense of moral and aesthetic outrage at the human spectacle. The theory of humours was a useful dramatic instrument, serving to clarify the comic character in its structural function. It derived from the contemporary psychological view that each man is ruled by a single "passion"; but, more deeply, it rested on the moral conviction that to surrender to one's "humour" is an abdication from reason: the "humorous" man elevates self above the rational design of God, and is therefore the legitimate object of satire.[2] Jonson's characters, like Marlowe's, are heroically obsessional: needing to become themselves to an absolute degree, they expose the raging vacuum of the self.

For a few years after 1598, Jonson's career was that of a young

[1] J. A. Barish, *Ben Jonson and the Language of Prose Comedy* (hereafter cited as *Barish*), p. 89. Cambridge (Harvard U.P.) 1960.

[2] See J. D. Redwine, "Beyond Psychology . . .", in *E.L.H.*, XXVIII (1961), pp. 316–34.

intellectual dramatist at war with his generation. In the angry experimental plays called "comicall satyres" (*Every Man Out Of His Humour, Cynthia's Revels, Poetaster*) he sought to bring the function of satire within the framework of comedy, notably by interposing a "Brechtian" commentator. For all their intelligence, these plays remain excessively self-conscious, and they wasted Jonson's time and energy in personal feuds. In 1603 he turned to tragedy, with *Sejanus*, a failure on the stage. This "tragicall satyre", on human lust for power, is in some ways allied to the mature comedies: there are links, for example, in poetic tone and imagery between the wooing of Livia by Sejanus[3] and of Dol by Mammon.[4]

Jonson's maturity as a comic dramatist came with *Volpone* (1605/6) and the plays which followed: *The Silent Woman* (1609/10), *The Alchemist* (1610), and *Bartholomew Fair* (1614). His later comedies were less happy, and his stature, supreme in its kind, rests on these four. Of them, *The Alchemist* is the most popular, the most engagingly comic, and on the stage still keeps its force.

Traditional criticism usually asserts that "Jonson is above all the realist. Comedies such as *The Alchemist* . . . are transcripts . . . of the daily life of London in the reign of James I".[5] This is obviously untrue; nobody on earth ever behaved like these creatures. This stress on "realism" is an echo of Jonson's claim to deal only in "deeds, and language such as men do use"; by this he meant that his plays moved in a recognisable world of experience, not one of irresponsible invention. But the critical approach through realism is self-terminating; after one has noted the accurate details, and exclaimed with Coleridge at the miraculous intricacy of the plot, there is no more to say. More recent critics have approached the plays as products of the poetic imagination, working through the discipline of poetic rhetoric, and have found their world to be, not one of antique eccentricity, but of permanent human experience.

*The Alchemist* is fundamentally concerned with the nature of man; alchemy is only its subject matter.[6]

---

[3] *Sejanus*, II. I.

[4] *The Alchemist* (the present edition, cited hereafter as *A*.), IV. I.

[5] *The Alchemist*, ed. C. M. Hathaway, p. iii. New York (Yale U.P.) 1903.

[6] E. B. Partridge, *The Broken Compass* (hereafter cited as *Partridge*), p. 238. London (Chatto and Windus) 1958.

The treatment of these subjects [*i.e.* alchemy and Jacobean behaviour] is no more realistic than is Bosch's portrait of a conjurer.[7]

Like *Volpone*, but with less bitterness, *The Alchemist* deals with human greed. Each of the gulls longs to possess that which the limit of his imagination encompasses. The miserable Drugger seeks only increased takings and a warm marriage. Dapper yearns to glitter at the local gaming house, and is so callow—so like a victim of the Victorian spiritualist D. D. Home—that he can accept the real presence of the Queen of Fairies.[8] The rancorous and oily Puritans, always a target for Jonson's rage, seek not only dishonest profits, but world power. Kastril is a naive oaf who longs to be a sophisticated bully. And towering over all like a comic Tamburlaine, lustful at bed and board, Mammon lets loose rapturous dreams wherein gold opens every lap and the belly swoons in more than Roman ecstasy.

This vision, rooted like the *Dunciad* in the London gutter, is created and sustained by Jonson's poetry. Because of their obsessions all his characters (except the null) talk endlessly. The language, belonging to them and to the poet, bears them along in a roaring flood of terms, derived from whatever jargon is relevant. Jonson's density of detail, based on exact observation, wide reading, and a fantastically accurate ear, has been often admired; but it is not merely an amassing of singulars—it is used dynamically to carry the play forward by a series of collisions between one self-regarding character and another. In this play several metaphorical systems operate. The alchemical is obvious, and there are animal parallels, as in *Volpone*. But the conspirators are also united in an "indenture tripartite", they form a "republic" with a "sovereign" (Subtle) and a "general" (Face); they also form a military "camp", with Dol as "cinque port". Their society, in fact, is an inversion and parody of organised living in its civil and military forms.[9]

---

[7] J. J. Enck, *Jonson and the Comic Truth*, p. 155. Madison (Wisconsin U.P.) 1957.

[8] Jonson was basing his fiction on fact. Thomas Rodgers was swindled in London about 1607 by just such a device; see J. T. McCullen, "Conference with the Queen of Fairies", in *S.N.*, XXIII (1950–1), pp. 87–95. There was another case in 1613/14; see K. M. Briggs, *The Anatomy of Puck*, p. 109. London (Routledge) 1959.

[9] See *Partridge* for a full analysis of imagery, and *Barish*, p. 79 ff. for a discussion of the relations and reactions of Jonsonian characters.

It is no coincidence that all these metaphorical systems occur also in alchemy. Its immense complexities are beyond present analysis, but in the debate between Subtle and Surly in II. III Jonson includes an admirably lucid exposition of its central thesis, namely, that all metals seek to become gold because all things in nature seek to perfect themselves.[10] By dramatic design, Subtle's alchemy is accurate and authentic, in terminology, theory, and practice. Jonson was attacking a real antagonist, not a remote and eccentric nuisance. Practical alchemy (which had attracted the attention of Chaucer in the *Canon's Yeoman's Tale*, Gower in *Confessio Amantis*, and Lydgate in *Secreta Secretorum*) had a long history. Sometimes it was respectable enough to gain royal patronage (Edward III and Raymond Lully), and always it drew rogues and fools. It received a new impetus in the 16th century from the "mineral physic" of Paracelsus; and in England the careers, glorious or not, of Dee, Kelley, and Forman were there for all to see, though it is not necessary to identify Subtle with any of them.

The newer writers tended to stress the symbolic element in the art—a point very relevant to this play. When seriously pursued, alchemy was not merely a search for gold. It was a component, if dubious, part of the "anagogical" system of thought universal in the Renaissance. The true alchemists were searching for God's hidden design in the natural world, and when they spoke in symbols they were asserting correspondences of the same kind as those acknowledged in politics and moral theology. Indeed, language belonging to almost any province of human experience can be used alchemically: birds, beasts, warriors, kings and queens, angels, dung, and cooking pots are all to be found. Sol and Luna, gold and silver, red and white, prefigure man and woman; substances are "married", "children" are born, and suffer illness, death, and resurrection. The stone, infinitely rare and so common that it can be picked up by the road-side, is also

---

[10] This section is an almost verbatim transcript of passages from the *Disquisitiones Magicae* of Martinus del Rio, 1599. Jonson made frequent use of this book, perhaps taking from it the idea of an alchemical "debate"; but it contains only a generalised account of the art, and for technical details he went to other books, like Geber's *Summa Perfectionis* and Arnoldus de Villa Nova's *Rosarium*. H.S. quote many relevant passages, which could be added to. The alchemists repeated themselves endlessly, and there were plenty of books available: Hathaway reckons that more than 113 appeared between 1595 and 1615.

a type of the risen Christ. There are far more glancing references of this kind scattered through the play than can be annotated.[11]

Jonson's object of attack was not a mere knavery, but a dangerous corruption of part of a respected system of thought and belief. Thus, the play is about transmutations which do not work, as alchemy does not work. Each of the gulls seeks to be changed from himself, but only becomes more completely what he really is. Subtle (*subtilis*, as of a liquid) is transformed from a picker-over of dung-hills to a velvet doctor, taking on in turn the irascible mask which greets the Puritans, or the gentle holy visage of the true-false hermit of Mammon's dream. In the end, a failed Faustus, he is exploded, vanishing *in fumo* over the back wall. With him goes Dol, smock-rampant, "common" as base earth, who has enjoyed transformation into Fairy Queen and baron's crazed daughter. Face is by turns captain, drudge, and almost a Spanish count: in the end relapsing into such self as he possesses as Jeremy the butler.[12]

In *Volpone* Jonson portrayed an enclosed world of evil, relieved only by two designedly ineffectual "good" characters. Surly and Love-wit are often thought to be the honest men of *The Alchemist*. Surly warns Mammon and refrains from seducing Dame Pliant; yet, on Mammon's evidence, he is not only a gamester, but a dishonest one.[13] Surly is more honest than Subtle and Face only because he is less ruthless; he envies them because he cannot compete. With Love-wit, who disentangles the knot in Act V as abruptly as any other *deus ex machina*, we meet the question that has concerned critics since Dryden: is it, in fact, "decorum", as Face claims in the close, that Love-wit should let him off? Love-wit, indeed, seduces Pliant (an ironically passive equivalent of the romantic heroine) and swindles Mammon. His role is surely made clear in his words to Jeremy, "I will be rul'd by thee in any thing". This is the standard concept of disorder, when "the baby beats the nurse", when servants disobey Lear, and "chaos is come again". Love-wit is a lord of misrule, though a genial one; only within the bounds of his amoral world is it "decorum" to forgive Face.

---

[11] *e.g.*, dungeon, III. III. 43; labyrinth, II. III. 308.

[12] I am reluctant to follow the more extreme analysis of C. G. Thayer, *Ben Jonson, Studies in the Plays* (hereafter cited as *Thayer*). Oklahoma (Oklahoma U.P.) 1963. In this view Subtle is the (bad) comic poet and Face the mercurial spirit of comedy itself; there is, in fact, alchemical justification for this approach.

[13] *A.*, II. I: cf. *Epigrams* 28, 82, for the associations of the name.

The circle is complete; the transformations leave men as they were; but the laughter that follows them into the streets of Blackfriars has a quality of ease.[14]

The play was entered on the Stationers' Register on 3 Oct. 1610, and was first performed, and presumably written, in that year. If we take literally Ananias' inconsistent calculations in III. II and v. v, they indicate (reckoning from March) a performance in October or November. But the plague was in London from 12 Jul. to 29 Nov., and there was an Oxford performance in September. It is therefore best to ascribe the composition and first performance to the period before July.[15]

On the Folio title-page Jonson placed a quotation emphasising the play's originality, and there is no need to look for a specific source, though no doubt he had read the *Canon's Yeoman's Tale* and Erasmus's brief *Alcumista*. Italian plays[16] had treated similar themes, but there is nothing to show that Jonson knew them. Dryden discovered a mare's nest when he announced that the play was based on Thomas Tomkis's adaptation of della Porta, *Albumazar*, a Cambridge play given in 1615, and Subtle on Albumazar himself.[17] Jonson did take some hints for his basic structure from Plautus' *Mostellaria*, in which slaves take over the house of an absent master and persuade him that it is haunted; one of Face's lines is a direct quotation.[18] Lyly had used alchemy in *Gallathea*, it is touched on in *Volpone*, and in 1616 Jonson made it the subject of the masque *Mercury Vindicated*.

In 1610 Lowin played Mammon, and Burbage, presumably, Face. The Court saw the play in 1613 and 1623, and public performances are known in 1631 and 1639. It was "played o'er and o'er", and after the Restoration became one of the "principal old stock plays". Pepys

---

[14] See A. Kernan, *The Cankered Muse*, for an analysis of Jonson's true-wit characters. New Haven (Yale U.P.) 1959.

[15] See *H.S.* IX, p. 224, cancelling their account in II, p. 87.

[16] Ariosto's *Negromante* (1520); Bruno's *Candelaio* (1582); della Porta's *Astrologo* (1606).

[17] See the edition by H. G. Dick, pp. 48 ff. for details. Los Angeles (California U.P.) 1944. Dryden was probably echoing inaccurate stage gossip. But I cannot agree with Dick and *H.S.* that there is no connection; Tomkis in fact used several phrases and jokes from Jonson which are not in the Italian.

[18] *A.*, v. II. 47, *cf.* l. 544 of *Mostellaria*. Thayer, p. 95, suggests also that Jonson remembered Aristophanes' *Plutus*.

found it "incomparable", though Aphra Behn observed a man sitting through it unmoved, with his hat on. After a gap in the records from 1675 to 1701, it was played regularly through the 18th century, and from 1743 till 1776 it was the preserve of Garrick in his star role as Drugger. Bell's edition of 1777 preserves the text of this version, in which Drugger's part is built up at the expense of dramatic balance. As Garrick's accounts show, the role was created with an extraordinary sense of imaginative detail, and it was only his skill which kept the play alive. When he let it go, there were only a few performances of Francis Gentleman's miserable two-act prose farce *The Tobacconist* (1771), the last (1815) featuring Kean. Thereafter, the play lapsed completely till 1899, when it was revived by Poel and the Elizabethan Stage Society. The Birmingham Rep. restored it to the professional stage in 1916, since when it has been given frequently.[19]

The staging, like the play, is highly concentrated. No upper level is used, and the comings and goings can be managed by the permanent stage entrances, with a window and perhaps one extra door. A problem arises in those scenes where some characters are inside and others outside the house. *H.S.*[20] and E. K. Chambers[21] visualise a wall built out on to the stage containing a door practicable from both sides, used by Face talking to Mammon in III. v—an arrangement found in *Henry VIII*, and elaborately in Heywood's *Golden Age*. If this is so, then every character entering from the street must be seen by the audience well before the entries implied in the text—Love-wit and the Neighbours, for instance, must appear, with nothing to say, before the end of IV. VII; and there are other difficulties. I have therefore followed the traditional editorial view[22] by which the stage turns itself into the exterior of the house for V. I–III, and probably III. I, but otherwise remains an interior, with the characters in the street heard, but not seen, "within".

---

[19] For full details see *H.S.*, IX, p. 223 ff.; R. G. Noyes, *Ben Jonson on the English Stage, 1660–1776*. Cambridge (Harvard U.P.) 1935. Also A. C. Sprague, "*The Alchemist* on the Stage", in *Theatre Notebook*, XVII (1962/3), pp. 46–7.

[20] *H.S.*, x, p. 49.

[21] *Elizabethan Stage*, III, p. 123.

[22] In effect re-stated by W. A. Armstrong, "Ben Jonson and Jacobean Stage-craft", in *Stratford-upon-Avon Studies*, I (1960), p. 58 ff.

# A NOTE ON THE TEXT

Along with *Sejanus* and *Volpone*, *The Alchemist* was entered on the Stationers' Register on 3 Oct. 1610, to Walter Burre, who brought out the quarto (Q) in 1612. Existing copies vary in the state of their quires.[1] Q shows characteristic signs of being based on Jonson's manuscript, especially in the peculiar scene-headings and the Jonsonian apostrophe ("I ga'you", "so'importunate"), by which he indicated the glides of natural speech while preserving some degree of metrical regularity. The corrections made in the Epistle show that he intervened personally during press-correction. Despite this, Q contains many errors and inconsistencies, especially in punctuation.

The authoritative text for Jonson's earlier plays is the folio of 1616 (F), the famous *Workes*. The present edition is based on F, in the B.M. copy C.39.k.9; I have also used a copy of my own, another in the Public Library, Auckland, and a microcard print of a copy in the New York Public Library.[2] There is no reason to question the traditional view that Jonson actively assisted Stansby in producing the volume, providing corrected and sometimes revised copy; de Vocht's attempts to elevate Q at the expense of F do not succeed. Jonson's intervention produces textual problems unlike those of other contemporary dramatists; there are few major cruces, but many difficulties of editorial consistency.

[1] See *H.S.*, v, pp. 275–6. I have used the B. M. Garrick copy (644.b.56), also available in the 1927 Noel Douglas facsimile, though this is frequently inaccurate. I have also consulted the B. M. Ashley copy, and H. de Vocht's edition of a Victoria and Albert copy in *Materials for the Study of the Old English Drama* XXIII. Louvain (Librairie Universitaire) 1950. This edition sometimes seems to rely on the misleading facsimile.

[2] *The Alchemist* occupies pp. 601–78, quires Eee–Lll 3v (wrongly signed Kkk). Its title runs: THE / ALCHEMIST. / *A Comœdie.* / Acted in the yeere 1610. By the / Kings MAIESTIES / Seruants. / The Author B. I. / LVCRET./— *petere inde coronam,* / *Vnde priùs nulli velarint tempora Musæ.* / [Rule] / LONDON, / Printed by WILLIAM STANSBY / [Rule] / M.DC.XVI./

The printing history of F has not yet been fully investigated.[3]
H.S.[4] thought that the copy went to printing in 1612/3, but Gerritsen
states that there is bibliographical evidence that the book was printed
1615/6, being completed in early summer 1616. Although some parts
contain heavy press-correction and re-setting, the printing of *The
Alchemist* was straightforward, and the collations in H.S.[5] show only
six minor variants. The Auckland and New York copies have a few
others, of no textual significance.[6] Apart from the rewriting of the
Dedication, the substantive changes made in F are slight—a few minor
revisions, the restoration of some brief omissions, and a few altera-
tions to satisfy the blasphemy law. But there are considerable changes
in other respects. Brackets and italics become comparatively consistent.
Punctuation, especially in the use of the final dash, is more accurate,
though it retains the character of combining grammatical and rhetorical
functions.[7] Q's passion for capitals is severely curbed—perhaps too
stringently, for in some places[8] a capital would be clearer. (Many are
restored in F2). By 17th-century standards, F is an accurate text, but not
even Jonson could completely overcome the inconsistency of his printers.

It seems that F was set up from a copy of Q revised and corrected
by Jonson. The common features cited by H.S.,[9] to which others
could be added, make this clear enough; and at II. III 221–2 H. Davis
shows that the confusion in line order arose because F was set up from
a copy of Q from which l. 221 had been omitted, and later written in.[10]
Copies lacking this line still exist. One may suppose that the copy of

---

[3] See J. Gerritsen, "Stansby and Jonson Produce a Folio. A Preliminary
Account", in *E.S.*, XLI (1959), pp. 52–5.

[4] H.S., IX, p. 14 ff.                           [5] H.S., IX, pp. 70–1.

[6] At I. III. 84 (p. 616) the Auckland copy has the uncorrected "too .DRV.",
other copies "too. DRV."; and on p. 674 the catchword "I may" is corrected in
the Auckland copy, and uncorrected, in the form "Imay", in other copies. The
New York copy has errors of pagination (619 not numbered, 656 as 665, 666
as 652, 667 as 657), and also the uncorrected "to" for "too" at v. II. 3 and "all"
for "all," at IV. IV. 8; other apparent variants are probably photographic.

[7] See especially the opening of I. III, where the rush of commas vividly
illuminates Drugger's nervous speech.

[8] *A.*, I. I. 17, *friers*; 25, *pie-corner*; 191, dagger.

[9] H.S., v, p. 278 ff.

[10] H. Davis, "Note on a Cancel in 'The Alchemist', 1612", in *The Library*
(5th series), XIII (1958), pp. 278–80; see textual note *ad loc.* The B. M. Ashley
copy originally had the leaf (E2) in this state, but this leaf is now in the Wrenn
copy in Texas.

Q used had been corrected in substantive readings, in brackets and punctuation, in some spellings, and probably in italicisation; but that for capitals the printer probably received only a general direction. To alter so many capitals would have produced almost illegible copy. Indifferent words are, of course, spelled with the usual freedom.

The second and fuller collected edition of Jonson's works (F2) came out in 1640, three years after his death, in two volumes. The first of these is a reprint of the 1616 volume, and there is nothing to show that the changes made in it have any textual authority. I have used copies in the British Museum and the Auckland Public Library. The third edition (F3) of 1692 was a reprint of F2, and for this I have mainly relied on the readings given in *H.S.*

In accordance with the general plan of this series, the text in this edition follows F very closely, varying from it only where, in my opinion, there is a definite error. All such variations are recorded in the textual notes. There are almost no stage directions in Q (the few which occur are indicated in the textual notes), but F has some 44 stage directions, printed in the margin opposite the relevant line. They are incomplete and irregular, but evidentially valuable. These directions have been reproduced at what seems the appropriate place, though this is not always quite certain because of their marginal setting. They have been left unchanged, except for capitalisation of proper names throughout, and except for the openings of III. v and IV. v, where they occur opposite the first line and have therefore been incorporated in the scene-headings. Stage directions in pointed brackets—⟨. . .⟩—are editorial. (Curved brackets, wherever used, are Jonson's. They indicate remarks which are in some sense outside the main flow of the dialogue. Often they are grammatical, but in many places equivalent to asides.)

Explanation is necessary as to the treatment of scene-headings. Jonson's "classical" system, based on Latin and continental precedent, is awkward and unhelpful. In *The Alchemist* the action is continuous, and, while an act-break indicates an empty stage, a scene-break means no more than a major entrance. Neither exits nor entrances are marked in Q or F with a very few irregular exceptions[11], and no indications of place are given. Each scene is headed solely by the names of the

---

11 These are, in F form: *Face returnes*; *He goes out*; *Face againe* (II. III); *Do; enters with a citterne* . . . (III. v); *They enter* (= *Exeunt*); *Mammon comes forth! They come forth*; *Drugger enters, and he beats him away* (= *Exit*) (V. v).

characters appearing in it, and the first speech, which never has a speech-heading, is spoken by the first-named character. Thus, at the opening of II. III, though Face is off-stage, F reads:

*Act* II. *Scene* III.

MAMMON, SUBTLE, SURLY, FACE.

Good morrow, father. SUB. Gentle sonne, good morrow. . . .

For ease of reading, all scene-headings (including the initial speech-heading) have been silently normalised, and any information given in them, though not bracketed, is editorial (except for III. v and IV. v, as noted above). Likewise, exits and entrances, though not given in F, have been normalised and left unbracketed[12]. Speech-headings have been normalised throughout, the full name being given.

The whole play is in verse. Where a line is divided between two or more speakers, F prints it as one line, inserting its usual abbreviated speech-heading, as in the example quoted. This edition follows normal modern practice by beginning each new speech on a new type-line, the verse-line being indicated by appropriate indentation. F is wholly inconsistent in its use of those stops which have separate italic and roman forms. I have used roman, except in lines which are wholly italic. Capitalisation has been standardised for names, and for the first two letters of each scene, where F has its own peculiar system. In accordance with the general practice of this series, the following changes from the original have been made without annotation: "and" for "&", short "s" for long "s", "i/j", "u/v", "w/vv" employed as in modern usage, and common abbreviations like "y$^r$" for "your" and "n̄" for "nn" expanded in full.

Textual Notes recording variants and emendations are to be found in two places; those variants significantly affecting meaning are recorded at the foot of the relevant page, all others are given scene by scene at the back of the book.

[12] Thus, "*Enter* SUBTLE", or "*Enter* SUBTLE, ⟨*with Spanish costume*⟩", means that there is no direction in F, while "*Enter* DOL *like the Queene of Faery*" means that F prints "*Dol like the Queene of Faery*".

## TO THE LADY, MOST
## DESERVING HER NAME,
## AND BLOUD:
### Mary,
## LA. WROTH.

MADAME,

*In the age of sacrifices, the truth of religion was not in the greatnesse, and fat of the offrings, but in the devotion, and zeale of the sacrificers: Else, what could a handfull of gummes have done in the sight of a* hecatombe? *or, how might I appeare at this altar, except with those affections, that no lesse love the light and witnesse, then they have the conscience of your vertue? If what I offer beare an acceptable odour, and hold the first strength, it is your value of it, which remembers, where, when, and to whom it was kindled. Otherwise, as the times are, there comes rarely forth that thing, so full of authoritie, or example, but by assiduitie and custome, growes lesse, and looses. This, yet, safe in your judgement (which is a* SIDNEYS) *is forbidden to speake more; lest it talke, or looke like one of the ambitious Faces of the time: who, the more they paint, are the lesse themselves.*

Your La:

true honorer,

BEN. JONSON.

# TO THE READER

*If thou beest more, thou art an Understander, and then I trust thee. If thou art one that tak'st up, and but a Pretender, beware at what hands thou receiv'st thy commoditie; for thou wert never more fair in the way to be cos'ned (then in this Age) in Poetry, especially in Playes: wherein, now, the Concupiscence of Daunces, and Antickes so raigneth, as to runne away from Nature, and be afraid of her, is the onely point of art that tickles the Spectators. But how out of purpose, and place, doe I name Art? when the Professors are growne so obstinate contemners of it, and presumers on their owne Naturalls, as they are deriders of all diligence that way, and, by simple mocking at the termes, when they understand not the things, thinke to get of wittily with their Ignorance. Nay, they are esteem'd the more learned, and sufficient for this, by the Many, through their excellent vice of judgement. For they commend Writers, as they doe Fencers, or Wrastlers; who if they come in robustuously, and put for it with a great deale of violence, are receiv'd for the braver fellowes: when many times their owne rudenesse is the cause of their disgrace, and a little touch of their Adversary gives all that boisterous force the foyle. I deny not, but that these men, who alwaies seeke to do more then inough, may some time happen on some thing that is good, and great; but very seldome: And when it comes it doth not recompence the rest of their ill. It sticks out perhaps, and is more eminent, because all is sordide, and vile about it: as lights are more discern'd in a thick darknesse, then a faint shadow. I speake not this, out of a hope to doe good on any man, against his will; for I know, if it were put to the question of theirs, and mine, the worse would finde more suffrages: because the most favour common errors. But I give thee this warning, that there is a great difference betweene those, that (to gain the opinion of Copie) utter all they can, how ever unfitly; and those that use election, and a meane. For it is onely the disease of the unskilfull, to thinke rude things greater then polish'd: or scatter'd more numerous then compos'd.*

# THE PERSONS OF THE PLAY

SUBTLE, *The Alchemist*

FACE, *The house-keeper*

DOL COMMON, *Their Colleague*

DAPPER, *A Clarke*

DRUGGER, *A Tabacco-man*

LOVE-WIT, *Master of the house*

EPICURE MAMMON, *A Knight*

SURLY, *A Gamster*

TRIBULATION, *A Pastor of Amsterdam*

ANANIAS, *A Deacon there*

KASTRIL, *The angry Boy*

DAME PLIANT, *His sister: A widdow*

NEIGHBOURS

OFFICERS

MUTES

*THE SCENE*, LONDON ⟨in LOVE-WIT's *house in Blackfriars, and the street outside.*⟩

# THE ARGUMENT

T *he sicknesse hot, a master quit, for feare,*
H *is house in towne: and one servant left there.*
E *ase him corrupted, and gave meanes to know*
A *cheater, and his punque; who, now brought low,*
L *eaving their narrow practise, were become*
C *os'ners at large: and, onely wanting some*
H *ouse to set up, with him they here contract,*
E *ach for a share, and all begin to act.*
M *uch company they draw, and much abuse,*
I *n casting figures, telling fortunes, newes,*
S *elling of flyes, flat bawdry, with the* stone:
T *ill it, and they, and all in* fume *are gone.*

# PROLOGUE

FORTUNE, that favours fooles, these two short houres
   We wish away; both for your sakes, and ours,
Judging Spectators: and desire in place,
   To th'Author justice, to our selves but grace.
Our *Scene* is *London*, 'cause we would make knowne,     5
   No countries mirth is better then our owne.
No clime breeds better matter, for your whore,
   Bawd, squire, impostor, many persons more,
Whose manners, now call'd humors, feed the stage:
   And which have still beene subject, for the rage     10
Or spleene of *comick*-writers. Though this pen
   Did never aime to grieve, but better men;
How e'er the age, he lives in, doth endure
   The vices that shee breeds, above their cure.
But, when the wholsome remedies are sweet,     15
   And, in their working, gaine, and profit meet,
He hopes to find no spirit so much diseas'd,
   But will, with such faire correctives be pleas'd.
For here, he doth not feare, who can apply.
   If there be any, that will sit so nigh     20
Unto the streame, to looke what it doth run,
   They shall find things, they'ld thinke, or wish, were done;
They are so naturall follies, but so showne,
   As even the doers may see, and yet not owne.

# ACT I

## SCENE I

*Enter* FACE *dressed as a captain,* SUBTLE *with a phial in his hand, and* DOL COMMON.

FACE. Beleev't, I will.

SUBTLE.            Thy worst. I fart at thee.

DOL. Ha'you your wits? Why gentlemen! for love—

FACE. Sirrah, I'll strip you—

SUBTLE.                  What to doe? lick figs
   Out at my—

FACE.         Rogue, rogue, out of all your sleights.

DOL. Nay, looke yee! Soveraigne, Generall, are you mad-men?     5

SUBTLE. O, let the wild sheepe loose. Ile gumme your silkes
   With good strong water, an'you come.

DOL.                    Will you have
   The neighbours heare you? Will you betray all?
   Harke, I heare some body.

FACE.            Sirrah—

SUBTLE.                  I shall marre
   All that the taylor has made, if you approch.     10

FACE. You most notorious whelpe, you insolent slave.
   Dare you doe this?

SUBTLE.           Yes faith, yes faith.

FACE.                   Why! who
   Am I, my mungrill? Who am I?

SUBTLE.              I'll tell you,
   Since you know not your selfe—

FACE.                Speake lower, rogue.

SUBTLE. Yes. You were once (time's not long past) the good,     15
   Honest, plaine, livery-three-pound-thrum; that kept
   Your masters worships house, here, in the *friers*,
   For the vacations—

FACE.           Will you be so lowd?

SUBTLE. Since, by my meanes, translated suburb-Captayne.

FACE. By your meanes, Doctor dog?

SUBTLE.                              Within mans memorie,          20
All this, I speake of.

FACE.                    Why, I pray you, have I
Beene countenanc'd by you? or you, by me?
Doe but collect, sir, where I met you first.

SUBTLE. I doe not heare well.

FACE.                         Not of this, I thinke it.
But I shall put you in mind, sir, at *pie-corner*,          25
Taking your meale of steeme in, from cookes stalls,
Where, like the father of hunger, you did walke
Piteously costive, with your pinch'd-horne-nose,
And your complexion, of the *romane* wash,
Stuck full of black, and melancholique wormes,          30
Like poulder-cornes, shot, at th'*artillerie-yard*.

SUBTLE. I wish, you could advance your voice, a little.

FACE. When you went pinn'd up, in the severall rags,
Yo'had rak'd, and pick'd from dung-hills, before day,
Your feet in mouldie slippers, for your kibes,          35
A felt of rugg, and a thin thredden cloake,
That scarce would cover your no-buttocks—

SUBTLE.                                   So, sir!

FACE. When all your *alchemy*, and your *algebra*,
Your *mineralls*, *vegetalls*, and *animalls*,
Your conjuring, cosning, and your dosen of trades,          40
Could not relieve your corps, with so much linnen
Would make you tinder, but to see a fire;
I ga'you count'nance, credit for your coales,
Your stills, your glasses, your *materialls*,
Built you a fornace, drew you customers,          45
Advanc'd all your black arts; lent you, beside,
A house to practise in—

SUBTLE.                    Your masters house?

FACE. Where you have studied the more thriving skill
Of bawdrie, since.

SUBTLE.              Yes, in your masters house.
You, and the rats, here, kept possession.          50
Make it not strange. I know, yo'were one, could keepe
The buttry-hatch still lock'd, and save the chippings,

Sell the dole-beere to *aqua-vitæ*-men,
The which, together with your *christ-masse* vailes,
At *post* and *paire*, your letting out of counters, 55
Made you a pretty stock, some twentie markes,
And gave you credit, to converse with cob-webs,
Here, since your mistris death hath broke up house.

FACE.　You might talke softlier, raskall.

SUBTLE.　　　　　　　　　　　　No, you *scarabe*,
I'll thunder you, in peeces. I will teach you 60
How to beware, to tempt a *furie*'againe
That carries tempest in his hand, and voice.

FACE.　The place has made you valiant.

SUBTLE.　　　　　　　　　　　　No, your clothes.
Thou vermine, have I tane thee, out of dung,
So poore, so wretched, when no living thing 65
Would keepe thee companie, but a spider, or worse?
Rais'd thee from broomes, and dust, and watring pots?
*Sublim'd* thee, and *exalted* thee, and *fix'd* thee
I'the *third region*, call'd our *state of grace*?
Wrought thee to *spirit*, to *quintessence*, with paines 70
Would twise have won me the *philosophers worke*?
Put thee in words, and fashion? made thee fit
For more then ordinarie fellowships?
Giv'n thee thy othes, thy quarrelling dimensions?
Thy rules, to cheat at horse-race, cock-pit, cardes, 75
Dice, or what ever gallant tincture, else?
Made thee a second, in mine owne great art?
And have I this for thanke? Doe you rebell?
Doe you flie out, i'the *projection*?
Would you be gone, now?

DOL.　　　　　　　Gentlemen, what meane you? 80
Will you marre all?

SUBTLE.　　　　　Slave, thou hadst had no name—

DOL.　Will you un-doe your selves, with civill warre?

SUBTLE.　Never beene knowne, past *equi clibanum*,
The heat of horse-dung, under ground, in cellars,
Or an ale-house, darker then deafe JOHN's: beene lost 85
To all mankind, but laundresses, and tapsters,
Had not I beene.

Dol.                 Do'you know who heares you, Soveraigne?
Face.  Sirrah—
Dol.                 Nay, Generall, I thought you were civill—
Face.  I shall turne desperate, if you grow thus lowd.
Subtle.  And hang thy selfe, I care not.
Face.                                     Hang thee, colliar,        90
    And all thy pots, and pans, in picture I will,
    Since thou hast mov'd me.—
Dol.                         (O, this'll ore-throw all.)
Face.  Write thee up bawd, in *Paules*; have all thy tricks
    Of cosning with a hollow cole, dust, scrapings,
    Searching for things lost, with a sive, and sheeres,        95
    Erecting *figures*, in your rowes of *houses*,
    And taking in of shaddowes, with a glasse,
    Told in red letters: And a face, cut for thee,
    Worse then GAMALIEL RATSEY'S.
Dol.                         Are you sound?
    Ha'you your senses, masters?
Face.                         I will have        100
    A booke, but barely reckoning thy impostures,
    Shall prove a true *philosophers stone*, to printers.
Subtle.  Away, you trencher-raskall.
Face.                                 Out you dog-leach,
    The vomit of all prisons—
Dol.                         Will you be
    Your owne destructions, gentlemen?
Face.                                 Still spew'd out        105
    For lying too heavy o'the basket.
Subtle.                         Cheater.
Face.  Bawd.
Subtle.          Cow-herd.
Face.                  Conjurer.
Subtle.                         Cut-purse.
Face.                                     Witch.
Dol.                                         O me!
    We are ruin'd! lost! Ha'you no more regard
    To your reputations? Where's your judgement? S'light,
    Have yet, some care of me, o'your *republique*—        110

FACE.  Away this brach.  I'll bring thee, rogue, within
　The *statute* of *sorcerie, tricesimo tertio*
　Of HARRY the eight: I, and (perhaps) thy necke
　Within a nooze, for laundring gold, and barbing it.
DOL.  You'll bring your head within a cocks-combe, will you?　115
　*She catcheth out* FACE *his sword: and breakes* SUBTLES *glasse.*
　And you, sir, with your *menstrue*, gather it up.
　S'death, you abominable paire of stinkards,
　Leave off your barking, and grow one againe,
　Or, by the light that shines, I'll cut your throats.
　I'll not be made a prey unto the *marshall*,　　　　　120
　For ne're a snarling dog-bolt o'you both.
　Ha'you together cossen'd all this while,
　And all the world, and shall it now be said
　Yo'have made most courteous shift, to cosen your selves?
　You will accuse him? You will bring him in　　　　125
　Within the *statute*? Who shall take your word?
　A whore-sonne, upstart, *apocryphall* captayne,
　Whom not a puritane, in black-*friers*, will trust
　So much, as for a feather! And you, too,
　Will give the cause, forsooth? You will insult,　　　130
　And claime a primacie, in the divisions?
　You must be chiefe? as if you, onely, had
　The poulder to project with? and the worke
　Were not begun out of equalitie?
　The venter *tripartite*? All things in common?　　　135
　Without prioritie? S'death, you perpetuall curres,
　Fall to your couples againe, and cossen kindly,
　And heartily, and lovingly, as you should,
　And loose not the beginning of a *terme*,
　Or, by this hand, I shall grow factious too,　　　140
　And, take my part, and quit you.
FACE.　　　　　　　　　　　　'Tis his fault,
　He ever murmures, and objects his paines,
　And sayes, the weight of all lyes upon him.
SUBTLE.  Why, so it do's.
DOL.　　　　　　　　How does it? Doe not we
　Sustaine our parts?

SUBTLE.                    Yes, but they are not equall.          145
DOL.  Why, if your part exceed to day, I hope
   Ours may, to morrow, match it.
SUBTLE.                    I, they may.
DOL.  May, murmuring mastiffe? I, and doe. Death on me!
   Helpe me to thrattell him.
SUBTLE.                    DOROTHEE, mistris DOROTHEE,
   O'ds precious, I'll doe any thing. What doe you meane?     150
DOL.  Because o'your *fermentation*, and *cibation*?
SUBTLE.  Not I, by heaven—
DOL.                    Your *Sol*, and *Luna*—helpe me.
SUBTLE.  Would I were hang'd then.  I'll conforme my selfe.
DOL.  Will you, sir, doe so then, and quickly: sweare.
SUBTLE.  What should I sweare?
DOL.                    To leave your faction, sir.     155
   And labour, kindly, in the commune worke.
SUBTLE.  Let me not breath, if I meant ought, beside.
   I onely us'd those speeches, as a spurre
   To him.
DOL.        I hope we need no spurres, sir. Doe we?
FACE.  'Slid, prove to day, who shall sharke best.
SUBTLE.                    Agreed.     160
DOL.  Yes, and worke close, and friendly.
SUBTLE.                    'Slight, the knot
   Shall grow the stronger, for this breach, with me.
DOL.  Why so, my good babounes! Shall we goe make
   A sort of sober, scirvy, precise neighbours,
   (That scarse have smil'd twise, sin'the king came in)     165
   A feast of laughter, at our follies? raskalls,
   Would runne themselves from breath, to see me ride,
   Or you t'have but a hole, to thrust your heads in,
   For which you should pay eare-rent? No, agree.
   And may *Don Provost* ride a feasting, long,     170
   In his old velvet jerken, and stayn'd scarfes,
   (My noble Soveraigne, and worthy Generall)
   Ere we contribute a new crewell garter
   To his most worsted worship.
SUBTLE.                    Royall DOL!
   Spoken like CLARIDIANA, and thy selfe!     175

FACE.  For which, at supper, thou shalt sit in triumph,
    And not be stil'd DOL Common, but DOL Proper,
    DOL Singular: the longest cut, at night,
    Shall draw thee for his DOL Particular.
SUBTLE.  Who's that? one rings. To the windo', DOL. Pray heav'n,  180
    The master doe not trouble us, this quarter.
FACE.  O, feare not him. While there dyes one, a weeke,
    O'the plague, hee's safe, from thinking toward *London*.
    Beside, hee's busie at his hop-yards, now:
    I had a letter from him. If he doe,                                185
    Hee'll send such word, for ayring o'the house
    As you shall have sufficient time, to quit it:
    Though we breake up a fortnight, 'tis no matter.
SUBTLE.  Who is it, DOL?
DOL.                                A fine yong quodling.
FACE.                                                            O,
    My Lawyers clarke, I lighted on, last night,                  190
    In *Hol'bourne*, at the dagger. He would have
    (I told you of him) a *familiar*,
    To rifle with, at horses, and winne cups.
DOL.  O, let him in.
SUBTLE.                        Stay. Who shall doo't?
FACE.                                                    Get you
    Your robes on. I will meet him, as going out.                 195
DOL.  And what shall I doe?
FACE.                        Not be seene, away.
                                    *Exit* DOL.
    Seeme you very reserv'd.
SUBTLE.                        Inough.
                                    *Exit* SUBTLE.
FACE.                                            God b'w'you, sir.
    I pray you, let him know that I was here.
    His name is DAPPER. I would gladly have staid, but—

## SCENE II

*Enter* DAPPER.

DAPPER.  Captaine, I am here.
  B

FACE.                    Who's that? He's come, I think, Doctor.
   Good faith, sir, I was going away.
DAPPER.                               In truth,
   I'am very sorry, Captaine.
FACE.                        But I thought
   Sure, I should meet you.
DAPPER.                        I, I'am very glad.
   I'had a scirvy *writ*, or two, to make,
   And I had lent my watch last night, to one
   That dines, to day, at the shrieffs: and so was rob'd
   Of my passe-time.

*Enter* SUBTLE, ⟨*wearing a doctor's velvet robe and cap.*⟩

                    Is this the cunning-man?
FACE.   This is his worship.
DAPPER.                    Is he a Doctor?
FACE.                               Yes.
DAPPER.   And ha'you broke with him, Captain?
FACE.                                    I.
DAPPER.                                    And how?   10
FACE.   Faith, he do's make the matter, sir, so daintie,
   I know not what to say—
DAPPER.                    Not so, good Captaine.
FACE.   Would I were fairely rid on't, beleeve me.
DAPPER.   Nay, now you grieve me, sir. Why should you wish
      so?
   I dare assure you. I'll not be ungratefull.                15
FACE.   I cannot thinke you will, sir. But the law
   Is such a thing—And then, he sayes, *Reade's* matter
   Falling so lately—
DAPPER.               *Reade?* He was an asse,
   And dealt, sir, with a foole.
FACE.                        It was a clarke, sir.
DAPPER.   A clarke?
FACE.               Nay, heare me, sir, you know the law   20
   Better, I thinke—
DAPPER.               I should, sir, and the danger.
   You know I shew'd the *statute* to you?
FACE.                                    You did so.

DAPPER.  And will I tell, then? By this hand, of flesh,
   Would it might never wright good *court*-hand, more,
   If I discover. What doe you thinke of me,            25
   That I am a *Chiause*?
FACE.                              What's that?
DAPPER.                                        The *Turke*, was here—
   As one would say, doe you thinke I am a *Turke*?
FACE.  I'll tell the Doctor so.
DAPPER.                           Doe, good sweet Captaine.
FACE.  Come, noble Doctor, 'pray thee, let's prevaile,
   This is the gentleman, and he is no *Chiause*.      30
SUBTLE.  Captaine, I have return'd you all my answere.
   I would doe much, sir, for your love—But this
   I neither may, nor can.
FACE.                        Tut, doe not say so.
   You deale, now, with a noble fellow, Doctor,
   One that will thanke you, richly, and h'is no *Chiause*:   35
   Let that, sir, move you.
SUBTLE.                       Pray you, forbeare—
FACE.                                        He has
   Foure angels, here—
SUBTLE.                    You doe me wrong, good sir.
FACE.  Doctor, wherein? To tempt you, with these spirits?
SUBTLE.  To tempt my art, and love, sir, to my perill.
   'Fore heav'n, I scarse can thinke you are my friend,   40
   That so would draw me to apparant danger.
FACE.  I draw you? A horse draw you, and a halter,
   You, and your flies together—
DAPPER.                            Nay, good Captayne.
FACE.  That know no difference of men.
SUBTLE.                                Good wordes, sir.
FACE.  Good deeds, sir, Doctor dogs-meate. 'Slight I bring you   45
   No cheating CLIM-*o'the*-CLOUGHS, or CLARIBELS,
   That looke as bigge as *five*-and-*fiftie*, and *flush*,
   And spit out secrets, like hot custard—
DAPPER.                                  Captayne.
FACE.  Nor any melancholike under-scribe,
   Shall tell the *Vicar*: but, a speciall gentle,      50

That is the heire to fortie markes, a yeere,
Consorts with the small poets of the time,
Is the sole hope of his old grand-mother,
That knowes the law, and writes you sixe faire hands,
Is a fine clarke, and has his cyphring perfect,                    55
Will take his oath, o'the *greeke* XENOPHON,
If need be, in his pocket: and can court
His mistris, out of OVID.

DAPPER.                    Nay, deare Captayne.

FACE.  Did you not tell me, so?

DAPPER.                    Yes, but I'ld ha'you
Use master Doctor, with some more respect.                    60

FACE.  Hang him proud stagge, with his broad velvet head.
But, for your sake, I'ld choake, ere I would change
An article of breath, with such a puck-fist—
Come let's be gone.

SUBTLE.                    Pray you, le'me speake with you.

DAPPER.  His worship calls you, Captayne.

FACE.                    I am sorry,                    65
I e're imbarqu'd my selfe, in such a businesse.

DAPPER.  Nay, good sir. He did call you.

FACE.                    Will he take, then?

SUBTLE.  First, heare me—

FACE.                    Not a syllable, 'lesse you take.

SUBTLE.  Pray ye', sir—

FACE.                    Upon no termes, but an *assumpsit*.

SUBTLE.  Your humor must be law.

*He takes the money.*

FACE.                    Why now, sir, talke.                    70
Now, I dare heare you with mine honour. Speake.
So may this gentleman too.

SUBTLE.                    Why, sir—

FACE.                    No whispring.

SUBTLE.  'Fore heav'n, you doe not apprehend the losse
You doe your selfe, in this.

FACE.                    Wherein? For what?

SUBTLE.  Mary, to be so'importunate for one,                    75
That, when he has it, will un-doe you all:
Hee'll winne up all the money i'the towne.

FACE.  How!

SUBTLE.         Yes. And blow up gamster, after gamster,
  As they doe crackers, in a *puppit*-play.
  If I doe give him a *familiar*,                                      80
  Give you him all you play for; never set him:
  For he will have it.

FACE.                 Y'are mistaken, Doctor.
  Why, he do's aske one but for cups, and horses,
  A rifling *flye*: none o'your great *familiars*.

DAPPER.  Yes, Captayne, I would have it, for all games.               85

SUBTLE.  I told you so.

FACE.                 'Slight, that's a new businesse!
  I understood you, a tame bird, to flie
  Twise in a *terme*, or so; on friday-nights,
  When you had left the office: for a nagge,
  Of fortie, or fiftie shillings.

DAPPER.              I, 'tis true, sir,                                90
  But I doe thinke, now, I shall leave the law,
  And therefore—

FACE.             Why, this changes quite the case!
  Do'you thinke, that I dare move him?

DAPPER.                         If you please, sir,
  All's one to him, I see.

FACE.             What! for that money?
  I cannot with my conscience. Nor should you                         95
  Make the request, me thinkes.

DAPPER.                 No, sir, I meane
  To adde consideration.

FACE.                 Why, then, sir,
  I'll trie. Say, that it were for all games, Doctor?

SUBTLE.  I say, then, not a mouth shall eate for him
  At any ordinarie, but o'the score,                                  100
  That is a gaming mouth, conceive me.

FACE.                     Indeed!

SUBTLE.  Hee'll draw you all the treasure of the realme,
  If it be set him.

FACE.          Speake you this from art?

SUBTLE.  I, sir, and reason too: the ground of art.

H'is o'the onely best complexion,                    105
The queene of *Fairy* loves.
FACE.                              What! is he!
SUBTLE.                                            Peace.
Hee'll over-heare you. Sir, should shee but see him—
FACE. What?
SUBTLE.        Do not you tell him.
FACE.                                  Will he win at cards too?
SUBTLE. The spirits of dead HOLLAND, living ISAAC,
You'ld sweare, were in him: such a vigorous luck      110
As cannot be resisted. 'Slight hee'll put
Sixe o'your gallants, to a cloke, indeed.
FACE. A strange successe, that some man shall be borne too!
SUBTLE. He heares you, man—
DAPPER.                        Sir, Ile not be ingratefull.
FACE. Faith, I have a confidence in his good nature:    115
You heare, he sayes, he will not be ingratefull.
SUBTLE. Why, as you please, my venture followes yours.
FACE. Troth, doe it, Doctor. Thinke him trustie, and make him.
He may make us both happy in an houre:
Win some five thousand pound, and send us two on't.    120
DAPPER. Beleeve it, and I will, sir.
FACE.                              And you shall, sir.
You have heard all?
DAPPER.              No, what was't? nothing, I sir.
FACE. Nothing?
DAPPER.        A little, sir.
                                    FACE *takes him aside.*
FACE.                            Well, a rare starre
Raign'd, at your birth.
DAPPER.                  At mine, sir? no.
FACE.                                      The Doctor
Sweares that you are—
SUBTLE.                Nay, Captaine, yo'll tell all, now.    125
FACE. Allyed to the queene of *Faerie.*
DAPPER.                                Who? that I am?
Beleeve it, no such matter—
FACE.                        Yes, and that
Yo'were borne with a caule o'your head.

DAPPER.                                    Who saies so?
FACE.                                                        Come.
  You know it well inough, though you dissemble it.
DAPPER.   I-fac, I doe not. You are mistaken.
FACE.                                           How!          130
  Sweare by your fac? and in a thing so knowne
  Unto the Doctor? How shall we, sir, trust you
  I'the other matter? Can we ever thinke,
  When you have wonne five, or sixe thousand pound,
  You'll send us shares in't, by this rate?
DAPPER.                              By JOVE, sir,            135
  I'll winne ten thousand pound, and send you halfe.
  I-fac's no oath.
SUBTLE.              No, no, he did but jest.
FACE.   Goe too. Goe, thanke the Doctor. He's your friend
  To take it so.
DAPPER.              I thanke his worship.
FACE.                                            So?
  Another angell.
DAPPER.              Must I?
FACE.                            Must you? Slight,            140
  What else is thankes? will you be triviall? Doctor,
  When must he come, for his *familiar*?
DAPPER.   Shall I not ha'it with me?
SUBTLE.                                O, good sir!
  There must a world of ceremonies passe,
  You must be bath'd, and fumigated, first;                  145
  Besides, the Queene of *Faerie* do's not rise,
  Till it be noone.
FACE.                    Not, if she daunc'd, to night.
SUBTLE.   And she must blesse it.
FACE.                                    Did you never see
  Her royall *Grace*, yet?
DAPPER.                          Whom?
FACE.                                        Your aunt of *Faerie*?
SUBTLE.   Not, since she kist him, in the cradle, Captayne,  150
  I can resolve you that.
FACE.                          Well, see her *Grace*,
  What ere it cost you, for a thing that I know!

It will be somewhat hard to compasse: but,
How ever, see her. You are made, beleeve it,
If you can see her. Her *Grace* is a lone woman,               155
And very rich, and if she take a phant'sye,
She will doe strange things. See her, at any hand.
'Slid, she may hap to leave you all she has!
It is the Doctors feare.

DAPPER.                    How will't be done, then?

FACE.   Let me alone, take you no thought. Doe you          160
But say to me, Captayne, I'll see her *Grace*.

DAPPER.   Captain, I'll see her *Grace*.

FACE.                            Inough.

                              *One knocks without.*

SUBTLE.                        Who's there?
Anone. (Conduct him forth, by the backe way)
Sir, against one a clock, prepare your selfe.
Till when you must be fasting; onely, take                   165
Three drops of vinegar, in, at your nose;
Two at your mouth; and one, at either eare;
Then, bath your fingers endes; and wash your eyes;
To sharpen your five senses; and, cry *hum*,
Thrise; and then *buz*, as often; and then, come.            170

FACE.   Can you remember this?

DAPPER.                        I warrant you.

FACE.   Well, then, away. 'Tis, but your bestowing
Some twenty nobles, 'mong her *Graces* servants;
And, put on a cleane shirt: You doe not know
What grace her *Grace* may doe you in cleane linnen.          175

                    *Exeunt* FACE *and* DAPPER.


                         SCENE III

SUBTLE.   ⟨*At the door.*⟩ Come in (Good wives, I pray you forbeare
    me, now.
Troth I can doe you no good, till after-noone)

*Enter* DRUGGER.

    What is your name, say you, ABEL DRUGGER?

DRUGGER.                                  Yes, sir.

SUBTLE.  A seller of *tabacco*?
DRUGGER.                        Yes, sir.
SUBTLE.                                        'Umh.
  Free of the *Grocers*?
DRUGGER.              I, and't please you.
SUBTLE.                                        Well——                    5
  Your businesse, ABEL?
DRUGGER.                This, and't please your worship,
  I'am a yong beginner, and am building
  Of a new shop, and't like your worship; just,
  At corner of a street: (Here's the plot on't.)
  And I would know, by art, sir, of your worship,          10
  Which way I should make my dore, by *necromancie*.
  And, where my shelves. And, which should be for boxes.
  And, which for pots. I would be glad to thrive, sir.
  And, I was wish'd to your worship, by a gentleman,
  One Captaine FACE, that say's you know mens *planets*,      15
  And their good *angels*, and their bad.
SUBTLE.                        I doe,
  If I doe see'hem——

*Enter* FACE.

FACE.              What! my honest ABEL?
  Thou art well met, here!
DRUGGER.                    Troth, sir, I was speaking,
  Just, as your worship came here, of your worship.
  I pray you, speake for me to master Doctor.              20
FACE.  He shall doe any thing. Doctor, doe you heare?
  This is my friend, ABEL, an honest fellow,
  He lets me have good *tabacco*, and he do's not
  Sophisticate it, with sack-lees, or oyle,
  Nor washes it in muscadell, and graines,               25
  Nor buries it, in gravell, under ground,
  Wrap'd up in greasie leather, or piss'd clouts:
  But keeps it in fine lilly-pots, that open'd,
  Smell like conserve of roses, or *french* beanes.
  He has his maple block, his silver tongs,              30
  *Winchester* pipes, and fire of juniper.
  A neate, spruce-honest-fellow, and no gold-smith.

SUBTLE.  H'is a fortunate fellow, that I am sure on—
FACE.  Alreadie, sir, ha'you found it? Lo'thee ABEL!
SUBTLE.  And, in right way to'ward riches—
FACE.                                        Sir.
SUBTLE.                                          This summer, 35
    He will be of the clothing of his companie:
    And, next spring, call'd to the scarlet. Spend what he can.
FACE.  What, and so little beard?
SUBTLE.                            Sir, you must thinke,
    He may have a receipt, to make haire come.
    But hee'll be wise, preserve his youth, and fine for't:   40
    His fortune lookes for him, another way.
FACE.  'Slid, Doctor, how canst thou know this so soone?
    I'am amus'd, at that!
SUBTLE.                      By a rule, Captaine,
    In *metaposcopie*, which I doe worke by,
    A certaine starre i'the fore-head, which you see not.   45
    Your chest-nut, or your olive-colour'd face
    Do's never faile: and your long eare doth promise.
    I knew't, by certaine spots too, in his teeth,
    And on the naile of his *mercurial* finger.
FACE.  Which finger's that?
SUBTLE.                      His little finger. Looke.   50
    Yo'were borne upon a wensday?
DRUGGER.                        Yes, indeed, sir.
SUBTLE.  The thumbe, in *chiromantie*, we give VENUS;
    The fore-finger to JOVE; the midst, to SATURNE;
    The ring to SOL; the least, to MERCURIE:
    Who was the lord, sir, of his *horoscope*,   55
    His *house of life* being *Libra*, which fore-shew'd,
    He should be a merchant, and should trade with ballance.
FACE.  Why, this is strange! Is't not, honest NAB?
SUBTLE. There is a ship now, comming from *Ormus*,
    That shall yeeld him, such a commoditie   60
    Of drugs—This is the west, and this the south?
DRUGGER.  Yes, sir.
SUBTLE.            And those are your two sides?
DRUGGER.                                        I, sir.

SUBTLE. Make me your dore, then, south; your broad side, west:
And, on the east-side of your shop, aloft,
Write *Mathlai, Tarmiel,* and *Baraborat*;                    65
Upon the north-part, *Rael, Velel, Thiel.*
They are the names of those *Mercurial* spirits,
That doe fright flyes from boxes.
DRUGGER.                              Yes, sir.
SUBTLE.                                        And
Beneath your threshold, bury me a load-stone
To draw in gallants, that weare spurres: The rest,          70
They'll seeme to follow.
FACE.                        That's a secret, NAB!
SUBTLE. And, on your stall, a puppet, with a vice,
And a court-*fucus*, to call city-dames.
You shall deale much, with *mineralls.*
DRUGGER.                              Sir, I have,
At home, alreadie—
SUBTLE.              I, I know, you'have *arsnike*,           75
*Vitriol, sal-tartre, argaile, alkaly,*
*Cinoper*: I know all. This fellow, Captaine,
Will come, in time, to be a great distiller,
And give a say (I will not say directly,
But very faire) at the *philosophers stone.*                 80
FACE. Why, how now, ABEL! Is this true?
DRUGGER.                              Good Captaine,
What must I give?
FACE.              Nay, Ile not counsell thee.
Thou hearst, what wealth (he sayes, spend what thou canst)
Th'art like to come too.
DRUGGER.              I would gi'him a crowne.
FACE. A crowne! 'nd toward such a fortune? Hart,            85
Thou shalt rather gi'him thy shop. No gold about thee?
DRUGGER. Yes, I have a *portague*, I ha'kept this halfe yeere.
FACE. Out on thee, NAB; S'light, there was such an offer—
'Shalt keepe't no longer, I'll gi'it him for thee?
Doctor, NAB prayes your worship, to drinke this: and sweares  90
He will appeare more gratefull, as your skill
Do's raise him in the world.

DRUGGER.                    I would intreat
   Another favour of his worship.
FACE.                         What is't, NAB?
DRUGGER.   But, to looke over, sir, my *almanack*,
   And crosse out my ill-dayes, that I may neither          95
   Bargaine, nor trust upon them.
FACE.                         That he shall, NAB.
   Leave it, it shall be done, 'gainst after-noone.
SUBTLE.   And a direction for his shelves.
FACE.                         Now, NAB?
   Art thou well pleas'd, NAB?
DRUGGER.           Thanke, sir, both your worships.
FACE.                              Away.

                                   *Exit* DRUGGER.

   Why, now, you smoky persecuter of nature!          100
   Now, doe you see, that some-thing's to be done,
   Beside your beech-coale, and your cor'sive waters,
   Your crosse-lets, crucibles, and cucurbites?
   You must have stuffe, brought home to you, to worke on?
   And, yet, you thinke, I am at no expence,          105
   In searching out these veines, then following'hem,
   Then trying'hem out. 'Fore god, my intelligence
   Costs me more money, then my share oft comes too,
   In these rare workes.
SUBTLE.              You'are pleasant, sir. How now?


                    SCENE IV

                    *Enter* DOL.

SUBTLE.   What say's, my daintie DOLKIN?
DOL.                         Yonder fish-wife
   Will not away. And there's your giantesse,
   The bawd of *Lambeth*.
SUBTLE.              Hart, I cannot speake with'hem.
DOL.   Not, afore night, I have told'hem, in a voice,
   Thorough the trunke, like one of your *familiars*.          5
   But I have spied sir EPICURE MAMMON—
SUBTLE.                         Where?

Dol.   Comming along, at far end of the lane,
 Slow of his feet, but earnest of his tongue,
 To one, that's with him.

Subtle.      Face, goe you, and shift,
 Dol, you must presently make readie, too—    10

Dol.   Why, what's the matter?

Subtle.      O, I did looke for him
 With the sunnes rising: 'Marvaile, he could sleepe!
 This is the day, I am to perfect for him
 The *magisterium*, our *great worke*, the *stone*;
 And yeeld it, made, into his hands: of which,    15
 He has, this month, talk'd, as he were possess'd.
 And, now, hee's dealing peeces on't, away.
 Me thinkes, I see him, entring ordinaries,
 Dispensing for the poxe; and plaguy-houses,
 Reaching his dose; walking *more-fields* for lepers;   20
 And offring citizens-wives pomander-bracelets,
 As his preservative, made of the *elixir*;
 Searching the spittle, to make old bawdes yong;
 And the high-waies, for beggars, to make rich:
 I see no end of his labours. He will make    25
 Nature asham'd, of her long sleepe: when art,
 Who's but a step-dame, shall doe more, then shee,
 In her best love to man-kind, ever could.
 If his dreame last, hee'll turne the age, to gold.

                *Exeunt.*


# ACT II

### SCENE I

*Enter* Mammon *and* Surly.

Mammon.   Come on, sir. Now, you set your foot on shore
 In *novo orbe*; Here's the rich *Peru*:
 And there within, sir, are the golden mines,
 Great Salomon's *Ophir*! He was sayling to't,
 Three yeeres, but we have reach'd it in ten months.    5
 This is the day, wherein, to all my friends,

I will pronounce the happy word, *be rich.*
This day, you shall be *spectatissimi.*
You shall no more deale with the hollow die,
Or the fraile card. No more be at charge of keeping          10
The livery-punke, for the yong heire, that must
Seale, at all houres, in his shirt. No more
If he denie, ha'him beaten to't, as he is
That brings him the commoditie. No more
Shall thirst of satten, or the covetous hunger             15
Of velvet entrailes, for a rude-spun cloke,
To be displaid at *Madame* AUGUSTA'S, make
The sonnes of *sword*, and *hazzard* fall before
The golden calfe, and on their knees, whole nights,
Commit idolatrie with wine, and trumpets:                  20
Or goe a feasting, after drum and ensigne.
No more of this. You shall start up yong *Vice-royes*,
And have your punques, and punquettees, my SURLY.
And unto thee, I speake it first, *be rich.*
Where is my SUBTLE, there? Within hough?

FACE.                                        (*Within*) Sir.   25
    Hee'll come to you, by and by.

MAMMON.                              That's his fire-drake,
    His lungs, his *Zephyrus*, he that puffes his coales,
    Till he firke nature up, in her owne center.
    You are not faithfull, sir. This night, I'll change
    All, that is mettall, in my house, to gold.               30
    And, early in the morning, will I send
    To all the plumbers, and the pewterers,
    And buy their tin, and lead up: and to *Lothbury*,
    For all the copper.

SURLY.                      What, and turne that too?

MAMMON.   Yes, and I'll purchase *Devonshire*, and *Cornwaile*,   35
    And make them perfect *Indies*! You admire now?

SURLY.   No faith.

MAMMON.            But when you see th'effects of the great med'cine!
    Of which one part projected on a hundred
    Of *Mercurie*, or *Venus*, or the *Moone*,
    Shall turne it, to as many of the *Sunne*;               40

                   II. I. 30. my] Q; thy F.

Nay, to a thousand, so *ad infinitum*:
You will beleeve me.
SURLY.                    Yes, when I see't, I will.
But, if my eyes doe cossen me so (and I
Giving'hem no occasion) sure, I'll have
A whore, shall pisse'hem out, next day.
MAMMON.                          Ha! Why?                    45
Doe you thinke, I fable with you? I assure you,
He that has once the *flower of the sunne*,
The perfect *ruby*, which we call *elixir*,
Not onely can doe that, but by it's vertue,
Can confer honour, love, respect, long life,                    50
Give safetie, valure: yea, and victorie,
To whom he will.  In eight, and twentie dayes,
I'll make an old man, of fourescore, a childe.
SURLY.  No doubt, hee's that alreadie.
MAMMON.                          Nay, I meane,
Restore his yeeres, renew him, like an eagle,                    55
To the fifth age; make him get sonnes, and daughters,
Yong giants; as our *Philosophers* have done
(The antient *Patriarkes* afore the floud)
But taking, once a weeke, on a knives point,
The quantitie of a graine of mustard, of it:                    60
Become stout MARSES, and beget yong CUPIDS.
SURLY.  The decay'd *Vestall's* of *Pickt-hatch* would thanke you,
That keepe the fire a-live, there.
MAMMON.                          'Tis the secret
Of nature, naturiz'd 'gainst all infections,
Cures all diseases, comming of all causes,                    65
A month's griefe, in a day; a yeeres, in twelve:
And, of what age soever, in a month.
Past all the doses, of your drugging Doctors.
I'll undertake, withall, to fright the plague
Out o'the kingdome, in three months.
SURLY.                          And I'll                    70
Be bound, the players shall sing your praises, then,
Without their poets.
MAMMON.              Sir, I'll doo't. Meane time,
I'll give away so much, unto my man,

Shall serve th'whole citie, with preservative,
Weekely, each house his dose, and at the rate—                    75
SURLY.  As he that built the water-worke, do's with water?
MAMMON.  You are incredulous.
SURLY.                              Faith, I have a humor,
I would not willingly be gull'd. Your *stone*
Cannot transmute me.
MAMMON.                     PERTINAX, SURLY,
Will you beleeve antiquitie? recordes?                            80
I'll shew you a booke, where MOSES, and his sister,
And SALOMON have written, of the art;
I, and a treatise penn'd by ADAM.
SURLY.                              How!
MAMMON.  O'the *Philosophers stone*, and in high-*Dutch*.
SURLY.  Did ADAM write, sir, in high-*Dutch*?
MAMMON.                              He did:                       85
Which proves it was the primitive tongue.
SURLY.                              What paper?
MAMMON.  On cedar board.
SURLY.                     O that, indeed (they say)
Will last 'gainst wormes.
MAMMON.                     'Tis like your *Irish* wood,
'Gainst cob-webs. I have a peece of JASONS fleece, too,
Which was no other, then a booke of *alchemie*,                   90
Writ in large sheepe-skin, a good fat ram-vellam.
Such was PYTHAGORA'S thigh, PANDORA'S tub;
And, all that fable of MEDEAS charmes,
The manner of our worke: The Bulls, our fornace,
Still breathing fire; our *argent-vive*, the Dragon:             95
The Dragons teeth, *mercury* sublimate,
That keepes the whitenesse, hardnesse, and the biting;
And they are gather'd, into JASON's helme,
(Th'*alembeke*) and then sow'd in MARS his field,
And, thence, sublim'd so often, till they are fix'd.            100
Both this, th'*Hesperian* garden, CADMUS storie,
JOVE's shower, the boone of MIDAS, ARGUS eyes,
BOCCACE his *Demogorgon*, thousands more,
All abstract riddles of our *stone*. How now?

## SCENE II

*Enter* FACE, *dressed as an alchemist's assistant.*

MAMMON.  Doe wee succeed? Is our day come? and hold's it?

FACE.  The evening will set red, upon you, sir;
 You have colour for it, crimson: the red *ferment*
 Has done his office. Three houres hence, prepare you
 To see projection.

MAMMON.                PERTINAX, my SURLY,                5
 Againe, I say to thee, aloud: *be rich.*
 This day, thou shalt have ingots: and, to morrow,
 Give lords th'affront. Is it, my ZEPHYRUS, right?
 Blushes the *bolts-head*?

FACE.                    Like a wench with child, sir,      10
 That were, but now, discover'd to her master.

MAMMON.  Excellent wittie *Lungs*! My onely care is,
 Where to get stuffe, inough now, to project on,
 This towne will not halfe serve me.

FACE.                          No, sir? Buy
 The covering of o'churches.

MAMMON.                That's true.

FACE.                                Yes.
 Let'hem stand bare, as doe their auditorie.              15
 Or cap'hem, new, with shingles.

MAMMON.                    No, good thatch:
 Thatch will lie light upo'the rafters, *Lungs*.
 *Lungs*, I will manumit thee, from the fornace;
 I will restore thee thy complexion, *Puffe*,
 Lost in the embers; and repaire this braine,             20
 Hurt wi'the fume o'the mettalls.

FACE.                    I have blowne, sir,
 Hard, for your worship; throwne by many a coale,
 When 'twas not beech; weigh'd those I put in, just,
 To keepe your heat, still even; These bleard-eyes
 Have wak'd, to reade your severall colours, sir,         25
 Of the *pale citron*, the *greene lyon*, the *crow*,
 The *peacocks taile*, the *plumed swan*.

MAMMON.                               And, lastly,
Thou hast descryed the *flower*, the *sanguis agni?*
FACE. Yes, sir.
MAMMON.            Where's master?
FACE.                               At's praiers, sir, he,
Good man, hee's doing his devotions,                    30
For the successe.
MAMMON.            *Lungs*, I will set a period,
To all thy labours: Thou shalt be the master
Of my *seraglia.*
FACE.            Good, sir.
MAMMON.                               But doe you heare?
I'll geld you, *Lungs.*
FACE.            Yes, sir.
MAMMON.                               For I doe meane
To have a list of wives, and concubines,                35
Equall with SALOMON; who had the *stone*
Alike, with me: and I will make me, a back
With the *elixir*, that shall be as tough
As HERCULES, to encounter fiftie a night.
Th'art sure, thou saw'st it *bloud?*
FACE.                     Both *bloud, and spirit*, sir.     40
MAMMON. I will have all my beds, blowne up; not stuft:
Downe is too hard. And then, mine oval roome,
Fill'd with such pictures, as TIBERIUS tooke
From ELEPHANTIS: and dull ARETINE
But coldly imitated. Then, my glasses,                  45
Cut in more subtill angles, to disperse,
And multiply the figures, as I walke
Naked betweene my *succubæ.* My mists
I'le have of perfume, vapor'd 'bout the roome,
To loose our selves in; and my baths, like pits         50
To fall into: from whence, we will come forth,
And rowle us drie in gossamour, and roses.
(Is it arriv'd at *ruby?*)—Where I spie
A wealthy citizen, or rich lawyer,
Have a sublim'd pure wife, unto that fellow             55
I'll send a thousand pound, to be my cuckold.
FACE. And I shall carry it?

MAMMON.                        No. I'll ha'no bawds,
  But fathers, and mothers. They will doe it best.
  Best of all others. And, my flatterers
  Shall be the pure, and gravest of Divines,                      60
  That I can get for money. My mere fooles,
  Eloquent burgesses, and then my poets,
  The same that writ so subtly of the *fart*,
  Whom I will entertaine, still, for that subject.
  The few, that would give out themselves, to be                  65
  Court, and towne-stallions, and, each where, belye
  Ladies, who are knowne most innocent, for them;
  Those will I begge, to make me *eunuchs* of:
  And they shall fan me with ten estrich tailes
  A piece, made in a plume, to gather wind.                       70
  We will be brave, *Puffe*, now we ha'the *med'cine*.
  My meat, shall all come in, in *Indian* shells,
  Dishes of agate, set in gold, and studded,
  With emeralds, saphyres, hiacynths, and rubies.
  The tongues of carpes, dormise, and camels heeles,             75
  Boil'd i'the spirit of SOL, and dissolv'd pearle,
  (APICIUS diet, 'gainst the *epilepsie*)
  And I will eate these broaths, with spoones of amber,
  Headed with diamant, and carbuncle.
  My foot-boy shall eate phesants, calverd salmons,              80
  Knots, godwits, lamprey's: I my selfe will have
  The beards of barbels, serv'd, in stead of sallades;
  Oild mushromes; and the swelling unctuous paps
  Of a fat pregnant sow, newly cut off,
  Drest with an exquisite, and poynant sauce;                    85
  For which, Ile say unto my cooke, there's gold,
  Goe forth, and be a knight.
FACE.                          Sir, I'll goe looke
  A little, how it heightens.
                                              *Exit* FACE.
MAMMON.                        Doe. My shirts
  I'll have of taffata-sarsnet, soft, and light
  As cob-webs; and for all my other rayment                      90
  It shall be such, as might provoke the *Persian*;
  Were he to teach the world riot, a new.

My gloves of fishes, and birds-skins, perfum'd
With gummes of *paradise*, and easterne aire—
SURLY.   And do'you thinke to have the *stone*, with this?          95
MAMMON.   No, I doe thinke, t'have all this, with the *stone*.
SURLY.   Why, I have heard, he must be *homo frugi*,
    A pious, holy, and religious man,
    One free from mortall sinne, a very virgin.
MAMMON.   That makes it, sir, he is so. But I buy it.          100
    My venter brings it me. He, honest wretch,
    A notable, superstitious, good soule,
    Has worne his knees bare, and his slippers bald,
    With prayer, and fasting for it: and, sir, let him
    Do'it alone, for me, still. Here he comes,          105
    Not a prophane word, afore him: 'Tis poyson.


### SCENE III

#### *Enter* SUBTLE.

MAMMON.   Good morrow, father.
SUBTLE.                                 Gentle sonne, good morrow,
    And, to your friend, there. What is he, is with you?
MAMMON.   An heretique, that I did bring along,
    In hope, sir, to convert him.
SUBTLE.                                 Sonne, I doubt
    Yo'are covetous, that thus you meet your time          5
    I'the just point: prevent your day, at morning.
    This argues something, worthy of a feare
    Of importune, and carnall appetite.
    Take heed, you doe not cause the blessing leave you,
    With your ungovern'd hast. I should be sorry,          10
    To see my labours, now, e'ene at perfection,
    Got by long watching, and large patience,
    Not prosper, where my love, and zeale hath plac'd'hem.
    Which (heaven I call to witnesse, with your selfe,
    To whom, I have pour'd my thoughts) in all my ends,          15
    Have look'd no way, but unto publique good,
    To pious uses, and deere charitie,

Now growne a prodigie with men. Wherein
If you, my sonne, should now prevaricate,
And, to your owne particular lusts, employ                    20
So great, and catholique a blisse: be sure,
A curse will follow, yea, and overtake
Your subtle, and most secret wayes.
MAMMON.                            I know, sir,
You shall not need to feare me. I but come,
To ha'you confute this gentleman.
SURLY.                        Who is,                          25
Indeed, sir, somewhat caustive of beliefe
Toward your *stone*: would not be gull'd.
SUBTLE.                        Well, sonne,
All that I can convince him in, is this,
The worke is done: Bright SOL is in his *robe*.
We have a *med'cine* of the *triple Soule*,                   30
The *glorified spirit*. Thankes be to heaven,
And make us worthy of it. Ulen ſpiegel.
FACE. ⟨*Within.*⟩ Anone, sir.
SUBTLE.                    Looke well to the register,
And let your heat, still, lessen by degrees,
To the *Aludels*.
FACE.            Yes, sir.
SUBTLE.                    Did you looke                       35
O'the *Bolts-head* yet?
FACE.                Which, on *D*. sir?
SUBTLE.                            I.
What's the complexion?
FACE.                Whitish.
SUBTLE.                            Infuse vinegar,
To draw his *volatile substance*, and his *tincture*:
And let the water in *Glasse E*. be *feltred*,
And put into the *Gripes egge*. Lute him well;              40
And leave him clos'd in *balneo*.
FACE.                I will, sir.
SURLY.  What a brave language here is? next to canting?
SUBTLE.  I'have another worke; you never saw, sonne,
That, three dayes since, past the *Philosophers wheele*,

II. III. 18. Now] F2, H.S.; No Q, F.

In the lent heat of *Athanor*; and's become                    45
*Sulphur o'nature.*
MAMMON.              But 'tis for me?
SUBTLE.                                        What need you?
You have inough, in that is, perfect.
MAMMON.                                        O, but—
SUBTLE. Why, this is covetise!
MAMMON.                            No, I assure you,
I shall employ it all, in pious uses,
Founding of colledges, and *grammar* schooles,                    50
Marrying yong virgins, building hospitalls,
And now, and then, a church.

*Enter* FACE.

SUBTLE.                            How now?
FACE.                                        Sir, please you,
Shall I not change the *feltre?*
SUBTLE.                    Mary, yes.
And bring me the complexion of *Glasse B.*

                                        *Exit* FACE.

MAMMON. Ha'you another?
SUBTLE.                    Yes, sonne, were I assur'd                    55
Your pietie were firme, we would not want
The meanes to glorifie it. But I hope the best:
I meane to tinct *C.* in *sand-heat*, to morrow,
And give him *imbibition.*
MAMMON.                    Of white oile?
SUBTLE. No, sir, of red. *F.* is come over the *helme* too,                    60
I thanke my Maker, in S. MARIES *bath*,
And shewes *lac Virginis.* Blessed be heaven.
I sent you of his *fæces* there, *calcin'd.*
Out of that *calx*, I'ha'wonne the *salt of* MERCURY.
MAMMON.   By powring on your *rectified water?*                    65
SUBTLE. Yes, and *reverberating* in *Athanor.*

*Enter* FACE.

How now? What colour saies it?
FACE.                                        The ground black, sir.
MAMMON. That's your *crowes-head?*

SURLY.                    Your cocks-comb's, is't not?
SUBTLE.   No, 'tis not perfect, would it were the *crow*.
   That worke wants some-thing.
SURLY.                    (O, I look'd for this.                    70
   The hay is a pitching.)
SUBTLE.                    Are you sure, you loos'd'hem
   I'their owne *menstrue*?
FACE.                    Yes, sir, and then married'hem,
   And put'hem in a *Bolts-head*, nipp'd to *digestion*,
   According as you bad me; when I set
   The *liquor* of MARS to *circulation*,                    75
   In the same heat.
SUBTLE.                    The processe, then, was right.
FACE.   Yes, by the token, sir, the *Retort* brake,
   And what was sav'd, was put into the *Pellicane*,
   And sign'd with HERMES *seale*.
SUBTLE.                    I thinke 'twas so.
   We should have a new *amalgama*.
SURLY.                    (O, this ferret                    80
   Is ranke as any pole-cat.)
SUBTLE.                    But I care not.
   Let him e'ene die; we have enough beside,
   In *embrion*. *H*. ha's his *white shirt* on?
FACE.                    Yes, sir,
   Hee's ripe for *inceration*: He stands warme,
   In his *ash-fire*. I would not, you should let                    85
   Any die now, if I might counsell, sir,
   For lucks sake to the rest. It is not good.
MAMMON.   He saies right.
SURLY.                    I, are you bolted?
FACE.                    Nay, I know't, sir,
   I'have seene th'ill fortune. What is some three ounces
   Of fresh *materialls*?
MAMMON.                    Is't no more?
FACE.                    No more, sir,                    90
   Of gold, t'*amalgame*, with some sixe of *Mercurie*.
MAMMON.   Away, here's money. What will serve?
FACE.                    Aske him,
                             sir.

MAMMON.  How much?

SUBTLE.                    Give him nine pound: you may
                                        gi'him ten.

SURLY.  Yes, twentie, and be cossend, doe.

MAMMON.                            There 'tis.

SUBTLE.  This needs not. But that you will have it, so,          95
    To see conclusions of all. For two
    Of our inferiour workes, are at *fixation*.
    A third is in *ascension*. Goe your waies.
    Ha'you set the oile of *Luna* in *kemia*?

FACE.  Yes, sir.

SUBTLE.          And the *philosophers* vinegar?

FACE.                                    I.          100

SURLY.  We shall have a sallad.

                                        *Exit* FACE.

MAMMON.                    When doe you make *projection*?

SUBTLE.  Sonne, be not hastie, I *exalt* our *med'cine*,
    By hanging him in *balneo vaporoso*;
    And giving him solution; then *congeale* him;
    And then *dissolve* him; then againe *congeale* him;          105
    For looke, how oft I iterate the worke,
    So many times, I adde unto his vertue.
    As, if at first, one ounce convert a hundred,
    After his second loose, hee'll turne a thousand;
    His third solution, ten; his fourth, a hundred.          110
    After his fifth, a thousand thousand ounces
    Of any imperfect mettall, into pure
    Silver, or gold, in all examinations,
    As good, as any of the naturall mine.
    Get you your stuffe here, against after-noone,          115
    Your brasse, your pewter, and your andirons.

MAMMON.  Not those of iron?

SUBTLE.                    Yes. You may bring them, too.
    Wee'll change all mettall's.

SURLY.                    I beleeve you, in that.

MAMMON.  Then I may send my spits?

SUBTLE.                            Yes, and your racks.

SURLY. And dripping-pans, and pot-hangers, and hookes?          120
  Shall he not?

SUBTLE.          If he please.

SURLY.                    To be an asse.

SUBTLE. How, sir!

MAMMON.          This gent'man, you must beare withall.
  I told you, he had no faith.

SURLY.                    And little hope, sir,
  But, much lesse charitie, should I gull my selfe.

SUBTLE. Why, what have you observ'd, sir, in our art,          125
  Seemes so impossible?

SURLY.                But your whole worke, no more.
  That you should hatch gold in a fornace, sir,
  As they doe egges, in *Egypt!*

SUBTLE.                Sir, doe you
  Beleeve that egges are hatch'd so?

SURLY.                    If I should?

SUBTLE. Why, I thinke that the greater miracle.          130
  No egge, but differs from a chicken, more,
  Then mettalls in themselves.

SURLY.                That cannot be.
  The egg's ordain'd by nature, to that end:
  And is a chicken in *potentia*.

SUBTLE. The same we say of lead, and other mettalls,          135
  Which would be gold, if they had time.

MAMMON.                    And that
  Our art doth furder.

SUBTLE.          I, for 'twere absurd
  To thinke that nature, in the earth, bred gold
  Perfect, i'the instant. Something went before.
  There must be remote matter.

SURLY.                I, what is that?          140

SUBTLE. Mary, we say—

MAMMON.          I, now it heats: stand Father.
  Pound him to dust—

SUBTLE.          It is, of the one part,
  A humide exhalation, which we call
  *Materia liquida*, or the *unctuous water*;
  On th'other part, a certaine crasse, and viscous          145

Portion of earth; both which, concorporate,
Doe make the elementarie matter of gold:
Which is not, yet, *propria materia*,
But commune to all mettalls, and all stones.
For, where it is forsaken of that moysture,                    150
And hath more drynesse, it becomes a stone;
Where it retaines more of the humid fatnesse,
It turnes to *sulphur*, or to *quick-silver*:
Who are the parents of all other mettalls.
Nor can this remote matter, sodainly,                         155
Progresse so from extreme, unto extreme,
As to grow gold, and leape ore all the meanes.
Nature doth, first, beget th'imperfect; then
Proceedes shee to the perfect. Of that ayrie,
And oily water, *mercury* is engendred;                       160
*Sulphure* o'the fat, and earthy part: the one
(Which is the last) supplying the place of male,
The other of the female, in all mettalls.
Some doe beleeve *hermaphrodeitie*,
That both doe act, and suffer. But, these two                 165
Make the rest ductile, malleable, extensive.
And, even in gold, they are; for we doe find
Seedes of them, by our fire, and gold in them:
And can produce the *species* of each mettall
More perfect thence, then nature doth in earth.               170
Beside, who doth not see, in daily practice,
Art can beget bees, hornets, beetles, waspes,
Out of the carcasses, and dung of creatures;
Yea, scorpions, of an herbe, being ritely plac'd:
And these are living creatures, far more perfect,             175
And excellent, then mettalls.
MAMMON.                              Well said, father!
Nay, if he take you in hand, sir, with an argument,
Hee'll bray you in a morter.
SURLY.                               'Pray you, sir, stay.
Rather, then I'll be brai'd, sir, I'll beleeve,
That *Alchemie* is a pretty kind of game,                     180
Somewhat like tricks o'the cards, to cheat a man,
With charming.

SUBTLE.                    Sir?

SURLY.                              What else are all your termes,
Whereon no one o'your writers grees with other?
Of your *elixir*, your *lac virginis*,
Your *stone*, your *med'cine*, and your *chrysosperme*,                    185
Your *sal*, your *sulphur*, and your *mercurie*,
Your *oyle of height*, your *tree of life*, your *bloud*,
Your *marchesite*, your *tutie*, your *magnesia*,
Your *toade*, your *crow*, your *dragon*, and your *panthar*,
Your *sunne*, your *moone*, your *firmament*, your *adrop*,                    190
Your *lato*, *aʒoch*, *ʒernich*, *chibrit*, *heautarit*,
And then, your *red man*, and your *white woman*,
With all your broths, your *menstrues*, and *materialls*,
Of pisse, and egge-shells, womens termes, mans bloud,
Haire o'the head, burnt clouts, chalke, merds, and clay,                    195
Poulder of bones, scalings of iron, glasse,
And worlds of other strange *ingredients*,
Would burst a man to name?

SUBTLE.                          And all these, nam'd,
Intending but one thing: which art our writers
Us'd to obscure their art.

MAMMON.                    Sir, so I told him,                    200
Because the simple idiot should not learne it,
And make it vulgar.

SUBTLE.                    Was not all the knowledge
Of the *Egyptians* writ in mystick *symboles*?
Speake not the *Scriptures*, oft, in *parables*?
Are not the choisest *fables* of the *Poets*,                    205
That were the fountaines, and first springs of wisedome,
Wrapt in perplexed *allegories*?

MAMMON.                          I urg'd that,
And clear'd to him, that SISIPHUS was damn'd
To roule the ceaslesse stone, onely, because
He would have made ours common.

                                        DOL *is seene.*
                              Who is this?                    210

SUBTLE.    God's precious—What doe you meane? Goe in, good
    lady,

Let me intreat you.

*Exit* DOL.

Where's this varlet?

*Enter* FACE.

FACE.                    Sir?
SUBTLE.   You very knave! doe you use me, thus?
FACE.                    Wherein, sir?
SUBTLE.   Goe in, and see, you traitor. Goe.

*Exit* FACE.

MAMMON.                    Who is it, sir?
SUBTLE.   Nothing, sir. Nothing.
MAMMON.                    What's the matter? good sir!   215
   I have not seene you thus distemp'red. Who is't?
SUBTLE.   All arts have still had, sir, their adversaries,
   But ours the most ignorant.
FACE *returns.*

What now?
FACE.   'Twas not my fault, sir, shee would speake with you.
SUBTLE.   Would she, sir? Follow me.

*Exit* SUBTLE.

MAMMON.                    Stay, *Lungs.*
FACE.                    I dare not, sir.   220
MAMMON.   Stay man, what is shee?
FACE.                    A lords sister, sir.
MAMMON.   How! 'Pray thee stay?
FACE.                    She's mad, sir, and sent hether—
   (Hee'll be mad too.
MAMMON.                    I warrant thee.) Why sent hether?
FACE.   Sir, to be cur'd.
SUBTLE.   ⟨*Within.*⟩        Why, raskall!
FACE.                    Loe you. Here, sir.

*He goes out.*

MAMMON.   'Fore-god, a BRADAMANTE, a brave piece.   225
SURLY.   Hart, this is a bawdy-house! I'll be burnt else.
MAMMON.   O, by this light, no. Doe not wrong him. H'is
   Too scrupulous, that way. It is his vice.
   No, h'is a rare physitian, doe him right.
   An excellent *Paracelsian*! and has done   230

215. good∧] H.S.; ~, F; Good∧ Q.

Strange cures with *minerall physicke*. He deales all
With *spirits*, he. He will not heare a word
Of GALEN, or his tedious *recipe's*.

FACE *againe*.

How now, *Lungs*!
FACE.                    Softly, sir, speake softly. I meant
To ha'told your worship all. This must not heare.                235
MAMMON.  No, he will not be gull'd; let him alone.
FACE.  Y'are very right, sir, shee is a most rare schollar;
And is gone mad, with studying BRAUGHTONS workes.
If you but name a word, touching the *Hebrew*,
Shee falls into her fit, and will discourse                       240
So learnedly of *genealogies*,
As you would runne mad, too, to heare her, sir.
MAMMON.  How might one doe t'have conference with her,
Lungs?
FACE.  O, divers have runne mad upon the conference.
I doe not know, sir: I am sent in hast,                           245
To fetch a violl.
SURLY.                    Be not gull'd, sir MAMMON.
MAMMON.  Wherein? 'Pray yee, be patient.
SURLY.                                    Yes, as you are.
And trust confederate knaves, and bawdes, and whores.
MAMMON.  You are too foule, beleeve it. Come here, Ulen.
One word.
FACE.          I dare not, in good faith.
MAMMON.                                    Stay, knave.         250
FACE.  H'is extreme angrie, that you saw her, sir.
MAMMON.  Drinke that. ⟨*Gives money.*⟩ What is shee, when shee's
out of her fit?
FACE.  O, the most affablest creature, sir! so merry!
So pleasant! shee'll mount you up, like *quick-silver*,
Over the *helme*; and *circulate*, like *oyle*,                   255
A very *vegetall*: discourse of *state*,
Of *mathematiques*, *bawdry*, any thing—
MAMMON.  Is shee no way accessible? no meanes,
No trick, to give a man a tast of her—wit—
Or so?—

SUBTLE. ⟨*Within.*⟩ Ulen.
FACE.                    I'll come to you againe, sir.          260

                                        *Exit* FACE.

MAMMON. SURLY, I did not thinke, one o'your breeding
   Would traduce personages of worth.
SURLY.                                   Sir EPICURE,
   Your friend to use: yet, still, loth to be gull'd.
   I doe not like your *philosophicall* bawdes.
   Their *stone* is lecherie inough, to pay for,          265
   Without this bait.
MAMMON.                    'Hart, you abuse your selfe.
   I know the lady, and her friends, and meanes,
   The originall of this disaster. Her brother
   H'as told me all.
SURLY.                    And yet, you ne're saw her
   Till now?
MAMMON. O, yes, but I forgot. I have (beleeve it)          270
   One o'the trecherou'st memories, I doe thinke,
   Of all mankind.
SURLY.                    What call you her, brother?
MAMMON.                                   My lord—
   He wi'not have his name knowne, now I thinke on't.
SURLY. A very trecherous memorie!
MAMMON.                                   O'my faith—
SURLY. Tut, if you ha'it not about you, passe it,          275
   Till we meet next.
MAMMON.                    Nay, by this hand, 'tis true.
   Hee's one I honour, and my noble friend,
   And I respect his house.
SURLY.                    Hart! can it be,
   That a grave sir, a rich, that has no need,
   A wise sir, too, at other times, should thus          280
   With his owne oathes, and arguments, make hard meanes
   To gull himselfe? And this be your *elixir*,
   Your *lapis mineralis*, and your *lunarie*,
   Give me your honest trick, yet, at *primero*,
   Or *gleeke*; and take your *lutum sapientis*,          285

               272. SURLY] SVB. Q, F.

Your *menstruum simplex*: I'll have gold, before you,
And, with lesse danger of the *quick-silver*;
Or the hot *sulphur*.

*Enter* FACE. ⟨*He speaks*⟩ *to* SURLY.

FACE.                    Here's one from Captaine FACE, sir,
Desires you meet him i'the *Temple*-church,
Some halfe houre hence, and upon earnest businesse.                    290

*He whispers* MAMMON.

Sir, if you please to quit us, now; and come,
Againe, within two houres: you shall have
My master busie examining o'the workes;
And I will steale you in, unto the partie,
That you may see her converse. ⟨*To* SURLY.⟩ Sir, shall I say,    295
You'll meet the Captaines worship?
SURLY.                              Sir, I will.
⟨*Aside.*⟩    But, by attorney, and to a second purpose.
Now, I am sure, it is a bawdy-house;
I'll sweare it, were the *Marshall* here, to thanke me:
The naming this Commander, doth confirme it.                    300
*Don* FACE! Why, h'is the most autentique dealer
I'these commodities! The *Superintendent*
To all the queinter traffiquers, in towne.
He is their *Visiter*, and do's appoint
Who lyes with whom; and at what houre; what price;    305
Which gowne; and in what smock; what fall; what tyre.
Him, will I prove, by a third person, to find
The subtilties of this darke *labyrinth*:
Which, if I doe discover, deare sir MAMMON,
You'll give your poore friend leave, though no *Philosopher*,    310
To laugh: for you that are, 'tis thought, shall weepe.
FACE.  Sir. He do's pray, you'll not forget.
SURLY.                              I will not, sir.
Sir EPICURE, I shall leave you?
MAMMON.                    I follow you, streight.

*Exit* SURLY.

FACE.  But doe so, good sir, to avoid suspicion.
This gent'man has a par'lous head.

MAMMON.                          But wilt thou, *Ulen*,          315
Be constant to thy promise?
FACE.                          As my life, sir.
MAMMON.  And wilt thou insinuate what I am? and praise me?
And say I am a noble fellow?
FACE.                          O, what else, sir?
And, that you'll make her royall, with the *stone*,
An Empresse; and your selfe king of *Bantam*.          320
MAMMON.  Wilt thou doe this?
FACE.                          Will I, sir?
MAMMON.                          *Lungs*, my *Lungs*!
I love thee.
FACE.          Send your stuffe, sir, that my master
May busie himselfe, about projection.
MAMMON.  Th'hast witch'd me, rogue: Take, ⟨*Gives money.*⟩ goe.
FACE.                          Your jack, and all, sir.
MAMMON.  Thou art a villaine—I will send my jack;          325
And the weights too. Slave, I could bite thine eare.
Away, thou dost not care for me.
FACE.                          Not I, sir?
MAMMON.  Come, I was borne to make thee, my good weasell;
Set thee on a bench: and, ha'thee twirle a chaine
With the best lords vermine, of'hem all.
FACE.                          Away, sir.          330
MAMMON.  A *Count*, nay, a *Count-palatine*—
FACE.                          Good sir, goe.
MAMMON.  Shall not advance thee, better: no, nor faster.

                                   *Exit* MAMMON.


                          SCENE IV

                   *Enter* SUBTLE *and* DOL.

SUBTLE.  Has he bit? Has he bit?
FACE.                          And swallow'd too, my SUBTLE.
I ha'giv'n him line, and now he playes, I faith.
SUBTLE.  And shall we twitch him?

FACE.                    Thorough both the gills.
  A wench is a rare bait, with which a man
  No sooner's taken, but he straight firkes mad.          5
SUBTLE.  DOL, my lord WHA'TS'HUMS sister, you must now
  Beare your selfe statelich.
DOL.                    O, let me alone.
  I'll not forget my race, I warrant you.
  I'll keepe my distance, laugh, and talke aloud;
  Have all the tricks of a proud scirvy ladie,          10
  And be as rude'as her woman.
FACE.                    Well said, *Sanguine.*
SUBTLE.  But will he send his andirons?
FACE.                    His jack too;
  And's iron shooing-horne: I ha'spoke to him. Well,
  I must not loose my wary gamster, yonder.
SUBTLE.  O *Monsieur Caution*, that will not be gull'd?          15
FACE.  I, if I can strike a fine hooke into him, now,
  The *Temple*-church, there I have cast mine angle.
  Well, pray for me. I'll about it.

                              *One knocks.*
SUBTLE.                    What, more gudgeons!
  DOL, scout, scout;          ⟨DOL *goes to the window.*⟩
                  stay FACE, you must goe to the dore:
  'Pray god, it be my *Anabaptist.* Who is't, DOL?          20
DOL.  I know him not. He lookes like a gold-end-man.
SUBTLE.  Gods so! 'tis he, he said he would send. What call you
    him?
  The *sanctified Elder*, that should deale
  For MAMMONS jack, and andirons! ⟨*To* FACE.⟩ Let him in.
  Stay, helpe me of, first, with my gowne.

                    *Exit* FACE ⟨*with the gown.*⟩

                  Away          25
Ma-dame, to your with-drawing chamber.
                    *Exit* DOL.
                  Now,
  In a new tune, new gesture, but old language.
  This fellow is sent, from one negotiates with me
  About the *stone*, too; for the *holy Brethren*
    C

Of *Amsterdam,* the *exil'd Saints:* that hope          30
To raise their *discipline,* by it. I must use him
In some strange fashion, now, to make him admire me.

### SCENE V

*Enter* FACE *and* ANANIAS.

SUBTLE.   Where is my drudge?
FACE.                            Sir.
SUBTLE.                            Take away the *recipient,*
   And rectifie your *menstrue,* from the *phlegma.*
   Then powre it, o'the *Sol,* in the *cucurbite,*
   And let'hem macerate, together.
FACE.                              Yes, sir.
   And save the ground?
SUBTLE.                  No. *Terra damnata*              5
   Must not have entrance, in the *worke.* Who are you?
ANANIAS.   A *faithfull Brother,* if it please you.
SUBTLE.                                What's that?
   A *Lullianist?* a *Ripley? Filius artis?*
   Can you *sublime,* and *dulcefie? calcine?*
   Know you the *sapor pontick? sapor stiptick?*          10
   Or, what is *homogene,* or *heterogene?*
ANANIAS.   I understand no *heathen* language, truely.
SUBTLE.   *Heathen,* you KNIPPER-DOLING? Is *Ars sacra,*
   Or *Chrysopœia,* or *Spagirica,*
   Or the *pamphysick,* or *panarchick* knowledge,        15
   A *heathen* language?
ANANIAS.              *Heathen Greeke,* I take it.
SUBTLE.   How? *heathen Greeke?*
ANANIAS.                    All's *heathen,* but the *Hebrew.*
SUBTLE.   Sirah, my varlet, stand you forth, and speake to him
   Like a *Philosopher:* Answere, i'the language.
   Name the vexations, and the martyrizations             20
   Of mettalls, in the worke.
FACE.                      Sir, *Putrefaction,*
   *Solution, Ablution, Sublimation,*
   *Cohobation, Calcination, Ceration* and
   *Fixation.*

SUBTLE.  This is *heathen Greeke*, to you, now?
 And when comes *Vivification?*
FACE.       After *Mortification.*  25
SUBTLE.  What's *Cohobation?*
FACE.       'Tis the powring on
 Your *Aqua Regis*, and then drawing him off,
 To the *trine circle* of the *seven spheares.*
SUBTLE.  What's the proper passion of mettalls?
FACE.        *Malleation.*
SUBTLE.  What's your *ultimum supplicium auri?*
FACE.       *Antimonium.*  30
SUBTLE.  This's *heathen Greeke*, to you? And, what's your
 *Mercury?*
FACE.  A very fugitive, he will be gone, sir.
SUBTLE.  How know you him?
FACE.      By his *viscositie*,
 His *oleositie*, and his *suscitabilitie.*
SUBTLE.  How doe you *sublime* him?
FACE.      With the *calce* of egge- 35
            shels,
 White marble, *talck.*
SUBTLE.    Your *magisterium*, now?
 What's that?
FACE.   Shifting, sir, your elements,
 Drie into cold, cold into moist, moist in-
 to hot, hot into drie.
SUBTLE.    This's *heathen Greeke* to you, still?
 Your *lapis philosophicus?*
FACE.      'Tis a *stone*, and not 40
 A *stone*; a *spirit*, a *soule*, and a *body*:
 Which, if you doe *dissolve*, it is *dissolv'd*,
 If you *coagulate*, it is *coagulated*,
 If you make it to *flye*, it *flyeth.*
SUBTLE.     Inough.

          *Exit* FACE.

 This's *heathen Greeke*, to you? What are you, sir? 45
ANANIAS.  Please you, a servant of the *exil'd Brethren*,
 That deale with widdowes, and with orphanes goods;

And make a just account, unto the *Saints*:
A *Deacon*.

SUBTLE.          O, you are sent from master WHOLSOME,
  Your teacher?

ANANIAS.          From TRIBULATION WHOLSOME,          50
  Our very zealous *Pastor*.

SUBTLE.                    Good. I have
  Some orphanes goods to come here.

ANANIAS.                              Of what kind, sir?

SUBTLE.  Pewter, and brasse, andirons, and kitchin ware,
  Mettalls, that we must use our med'cine on:
  Wherein the *Brethren* may have a penn'orth.          55
  For readie money.

ANANIAS.          Were the orphanes parents
  *Sincere professors?*

SUBTLE.          Why doe you aske?

ANANIAS.                              Because
  We then are to deale justly, and give (in truth)
  Their utmost valew.

SUBTLE.                    'Slid, you'ld cossen, else,
  And if their parents were not of the *faithfull?*          60
  I will not trust you, now I thinke on't,
  Till I ha'talk'd with your *Pastor*. Ha'you brought money
  To buy more coales?

ANANIAS.          No, surely.

SUBTLE.                    No? How so?

ANANIAS.  The *Brethren* bid me say unto you, sir.
  Surely, they will not venter any more,          65
  Till they may see *projection*.

SUBTLE.                    How!

ANANIAS.                    Yo'have had,
  For the *instruments*, as bricks, and lome, and glasses,
  Alreadie thirtie pound; and, for *materialls*,
  They say, some ninetie more: And, they have heard, since,
  That one, at *Heidelberg*, made it, of an egge,          70
  And a small paper of pin-dust.

SUBTLE.                    What's your name?

ANANIAS.  My name is ANANIAS.

SUBTLE.　　　　　　　　　　　　Out, the varlet
　　That cossend the *Apostles*! Hence, away,
　　Flee *Mischiefe*; had your *holy Consistorie*
　　No name to send me, of another sound;　　　　　　　　　75
　　Then wicked ANANIAS? Send your *Elders*,
　　Hither, to make atonement for you, quickly.
　　And gi'me satisfaction; or out goes
　　The fire: and downe th'*alembekes*, and the fornace.
　　*Piger Henricus*, or what not. Thou wretch,　　　　　　80
　　Both *Sericon*, and *Bufo*, shall be lost,
　　Tell'hem. All hope of rooting out the *Bishops*,
　　Or th'*Antichristian Hierarchie* shall perish,
　　If they stay threescore minutes. The *Aqueitie*,
　　*Terreitie*, and *Sulphureitie*　　　　　　　　　　　85
　　Shall runne together againe, and all be annull'd
　　Thou wicked ANANIAS.

　　　　　　　　　　　　　　　　　*Exit* ANANIAS.

　　　　　　　　　This will fetch'hem,
　　And make'hem hast towards their gulling more.
　　A man must deale like a rough nurse, and fright
　　Those, that are froward, to an appetite.　　　　　　　90

### SCENE VI

### *Enter* FACE *and* DRUGGER.

FACE.　H'is busie with his spirits, but wee'll upon him.
SUBTLE.　How now! What mates? What *Baiards* ha'wee here?
FACE.　I told you, he would be furious. Sir, here's NAB,
　　Has brought yo'another piece of gold, to looke on:
　　(We must appease him. Give it me) and prayes you,　　5
　　You would devise (what is it NAB?)
DRUGGER.　　　　　　　　　　　　A signe, sir.
FACE.　I, a good lucky one, a thriving signe, Doctor.
SUBTLE.　I was devising now.
FACE.　　　　　　　　　　　('Slight, doe not say so,
　　He will repent he ga'you any more.)
　　What say you to his *constellation*, Doctor?　　　　　10
　　The *Ballance*?

　　　　　II. V. 78 out goes] Q; out-goes F, H.S.

SUBTLE.          No, that way is stale, and common.
   A townes-man, borne in *Taurus*, gives the bull;
   Or the bulls-head: In *Aries*, the ram.
   A poore device. No, I will have his name
   Form'd in some mystick character; whose *radii*,          15
   Striking the senses of the passers by,
   Shall, by a vertuall influence, breed affections,
   That may result upon the partie ownes it:
   As thus—
FACE.          NAB!
SUBTLE.                    He first shall have a bell, that's ABEL;
   And, by it, standing one, whose name is DEE,          20
   In a rugg gowne; there's *D*. and *Rug*, that's DRUG:
   And, right anenst him, a Dog snarling *Er*;
   There's DRUGGER, ABEL DRUGGER. That's his signe.
   And here's now *mysterie*, and *hieroglyphick*!
FACE. ABEL, thou art made.
DRUGGER. ⟨*Bows.*⟩          Sir, I doe thanke his worship.          25
FACE. Sixe o'thy legs more, will not doe it, NAB.
   He has brought you a pipe of *tabacco*, Doctor.
DRUGGER.                    Yes, sir:
   I have another thing, I would impart—
FACE. Out with it, NAB.
DRUGGER.          Sir, there is lodg'd, hard by me,
   A rich yong widdow—
FACE.          Good! a *bona roba*?          30
DRUGGER. But nineteene, at the most.
FACE.                    Very good, ABEL.
DRUGGER. Mary, sh'is not in fashion, yet; shee weares
   A hood: but't stands a cop.
FACE.                    No matter, ABEL.
DRUGGER. And, I doe, now and then give her a *fucus*—
FACE. What! dost thou deale, NAB?
SUBTLE.                    I did tell you, Captaine.          35
DRUGGER. And physick too sometime, sir: for which shee trusts
   me
   With all her mind. Shee's come up here, of purpose
   To learne the fashion.
FACE.                    Good (his match too!) on, NAB.

DRUGGER.   And shee do's strangely long to know her fortune.
FACE.   Gods lid, NAB, send her to the Doctor, hether.                    40
DRUGGER.   Yes, I have spoke to her of his worship, alreadie:
  But shee's afraid, it will be blowne abroad
  And hurt her marriage.
FACE.                        Hurt it? 'Tis the way
  To heale it, if 'twere hurt; to make it more
  Follow'd, and sought: NAB, thou shalt tell her this.                    45
  Shee'll be more knowne, more talk'd of, and your widdowes
  Are ne'er of any price till they be famous;
  Their honour is their multitude of sutors:
  Send her, it may be thy good fortune. What?
  Thou dost not know.
DRUGGER.                 No, sir, shee'll never marry                     50
  Under a knight. Her brother has made a vow.
FACE.   What, and dost thou despaire, my little NAB,
  Knowing, what the Doctor has set downe for thee,
  And, seeing so many, o'the citie, dub'd?
  One glasse o'thy water, with a *Madame*, I know,                        55
  Will have it done, NAB. What's her brother? a knight?
DRUGGER.   No, sir, a gentleman, newly warme in'his land, sir,
  Scarse cold in his one and twentie; that do's governe
  His sister, here: and is a man himselfe
  Of some three thousand a yeere, and is come up                         60
  To learne to quarrell, and to live by his wits,
  And will goe downe againe, and dye i'the countrey.
FACE.   How! to quarrell?
DRUGGER.                   Yes, sir, to carry quarrells,
  As gallants doe, and manage'hem, by line.
FACE.   'Slid, NAB! The Doctor is the onely man                          65
  In *Christendome* for him. He has made a table,
  With *Mathematicall* demonstrations,
  Touching the Art of quarrells. He will give him
  An instrument to quarrell by. Goe, bring'hem, both:
  Him, and his sister. And, for thee, with her                           70
  The Doctor happ'ly may perswade. Goe to.
  'Shalt give his worship, a new damaske suite
  Upon the premisses.
SUBTLE.                 O, good Captaine.

FACE.                                   He shall,
  He is the honestest fellow, Doctor. Stay not,
  No offers, bring the damaske, and the parties.                      75
DRUGGER.  I'll trie my power, sir.
FACE.                            And thy will too, NAB.
SUBTLE.  'Tis good *tabacco* this! What is't an ounce?
FACE.  He'll send you a pound, Doctor.
SUBTLE.                              O, no.
FACE.                                   He will do't.
  It is the gooddest soule. ABEL, about it.
  (Thou shalt know more anone. Away, be gone.)                       80

                                         *Exit* DRUGGER.

  A miserable rogue, and lives with cheese,
  And has the wormes. That was the cause indeed
  Why he came now. He dealt with me, in private,
  To get a med'cine for'hem.
SUBTLE.                      And shall, sir. This workes.
FACE.  A wife, a wife, for one on'us, my deare SUBTLE:           85
  Wee'll eene draw lots, and he, that failes, shall have
  The more in goods, the other has in taile.
SUBTLE.  Rather the lesse. For shee may be so light
  She may want graines.
FACE.                  I, or be such a burden,
  A man would scarse endure her, for the whole.               90
SUBTLE.  Faith, best let's see her first, and then determine.
FACE.  Content. But DOL must ha'no breath on't.
SUBTLE.                                   Mum.
  Away, you to your SURLY yonder, catch him.
FACE.  'Pray god, I ha'not stai'd too long.
SUBTLE.                              I feare it.
                                              *Exeunt.*

# ACT III

## SCENE I

*Enter* TRIBULATION *and* ANANIAS.

TRIBULATION.  These chastisements are common to the *Saints*,
  And such rebukes we of the *Separation*
  Must beare, with willing shoulders, as the trialls
  Sent forth, to tempt our frailties.
ANANIAS.                          In pure zeale,
  I doe not like the man: He is a *heathen*.                        5
  And speakes the language of *Canaan*, truely.
TRIBULATION.  I thinke him a prophane person, indeed.
ANANIAS.                                          He beares
  The visible marke of the *Beast*, in his fore-head.
  And for his *Stone*, it is a worke of darknesse,
  And, with *Philosophie*, blinds the eyes of man.              10
TRIBULATION.  Good *Brother*, we must bend unto all meanes,
  That may give furtherance, to the *holy cause*.
ANANIAS.  Which his cannot: The *sanctified cause*
  Should have a *sanctified course*.
TRIBULATION.                          Not alwaies necessary.
  The children of perdition are, oft-times,                          15
  Made instruments even of the greatest workes.
  Beside, we should give somewhat to mans nature,
  The place he lives in, still about the fire,
  And fume of mettalls, that intoxicate
  The braine of man, and make him prone to passion.          20
  Where have you greater *Atheists*, then your Cookes?
  Or more prophane, or cholerick then your Glasse-men?
  More *Antichristian*, then your Bell-founders?
  What makes the Devill so devillish, I would aske you,
  *Sathan*, our common enemie, but his being                        25
  Perpetually about the fire, and boyling
  *Brimstone*, and *arsnike*? We must give, I say,
  Unto the motives, and the stirrers up
  Of humours in the bloud. It may be so,

> III. I. 29. SO,] H.S.; ~. Q^u, F; ~; Q^c.

When as the *worke* is done, the *stone* is made,                    30
This heate of his may turne into a zeale,
And stand up for the *beauteous discipline*,
Against the menstruous cloth, and ragg of *Rome*.
We must await his calling, and the comming
Of the good spirit. You did fault, t'upbraid him                    35
With the *Brethrens* blessing of *Heidelberg*, waighing
What need we have, to hasten on the worke,
For the restoring of the *silenc'd Saints*,
Which ne'er will be, but by the *Philosophers stone*.
And, so a learned *Elder*, one of *Scotland*,                       40
Assur'd me; *Aurum potabile* being
The onely med'cine, for the civill *Magistrate*,
T'incline him to a feeling of the cause:
And must be daily us'd, in the disease.
ANANIAS.  I have not edified more, truely, by man;                  45
Not, since the *beautifull light*, first, shone on me:
And I am sad, my zeale hath so offended.
TRIBULATION.  Let us call on him, then.
ANANIAS.                                    The motion's good,
And of the spirit; I will knock first: Peace be within.
                                              ⟨*He knocks.*⟩


SCENE II

*Enter* SUBTLE.

SUBTLE.  O, are you come? 'Twas time. Your threescore minutes
    Were at the last thred, you see ⟨*Shows hour-glass.*⟩; and downe
        had gone
    *Furnus acediæ, Turris circulatorius*:
    *Lembeke, Bolts-head, Retort*, and *Pellicane*
    Had all beene cinders. Wicked ANANIAS!                          5
    Art thou return'd? Nay then, it goes downe, yet.
TRIBULATION.  Sir, be appeased, he is come to humble
    Himselfe in spirit, and to aske your patience,
    If too much zeale hath carried him, aside,
    From the due path.
SUBTLE.                        Why, this doth qualifie!             10

TRIBULATION.  The *Brethren* had no purpose, verely,
   To give you the least grievance: but are ready
   To lend their willing hands, to any project
   The spirit, and you direct.
SUBTLE.                              This qualifies more!
TRIBULATION.  And, for the orphanes goods, let them be valew'd,   15
   Or what is needfull, else, to the holy worke,
   It shall be numbred: here, by me, the *Saints*
   Throw downe their purse before you.
SUBTLE.                              This qualifies, most!
   Why, thus it should be, now you understand.
   Have I discours'd so unto you, of our *Stone*?       20
   And, of the good that it shall bring your cause?
   Shew'd you, (beside the mayne of hiring forces
   Abroad, drawing the *Hollanders*, your friends,
   From th'*Indies*, to serve you, with all their fleete)
   That even the med'cinall use shall make you a faction,   25
   And party in the realme? As, put the case,
   That some great man in state, he have the gout,
   Why, you but send three droppes of your *Elixir*,
   You helpe him straight: there you have made a friend.
   Another has the palsey, or the dropsie,       30
   He takes of your incombustible stuffe,
   Hee's yong againe: there you have made a friend.
   A Lady, that is past the feate of body,
   Though not of minde, and hath her face decay'd
   Beyond all cure of paintings, you restore      35
   With the oyle of *Talck*; there you have made a friend:
   And all her friends. A lord, that is a *Leper*,
   A knight, that has the bone-ache, or a squire
   That hath both these, you make'hem smooth, and sound,
   With a bare *fricace* of your med'cine: still,     40
   You increase your friends.
TRIBULATION.                   I, 'tis very pregnant.
SUBTLE.  And, then, the turning of this Lawyers pewter
   To plate, at *Christ-masse*—
ANANIAS.                       *Christ-tide*, I pray you.
SUBTLE.  Yet, ANANIAS?
ANANIAS.                I have done.

SUBTLE.                                    Or changing
  His parcell guilt, to massie gold. You cannot                    45
  But raise you friends. Withall, to be of power
  To pay an armie, in the field, to buy
  The king of *France*, out of his realmes; or *Spaine*,
  Out of his *Indies*: What can you not doe,
  Against lords spirituall, or temporall,                    50
  That shall oppone you?
TRIBULATION.                    Verily, 'tis true.
  We may be temporall lords, our selves, I take it.
SUBTLE.  You may be any thing, and leave off to make
  Long-winded exercises: or suck up,
  Your ha, and hum, in a tune. I not denie,                    55
  But such as are not graced, in a state,
  May, for their ends, be adverse in religion,
  And get a tune, to call the flock together:
  For (to say sooth) a tune do's much, with women,
  And other phlegmatick people, it is your bell.                    60
ANANIAS.  Bells are prophane: a tune may be religious.
SUBTLE.  No warning with you? Then, farewell my patience.
  'Slight, it shall downe: I will not be thus tortur'd.
TRIBULATION.  I pray you, sir.
SUBTLE.                    All shall perish. I have spoke it.
TRIBULATION.  Let me find grace, sir, in your eyes; the man                    65
  He stands corrected: neither did his zeale
  (But as your selfe) allow a tune, some-where.
  Which, now, being to'ard the stone, we shall not need.
SUBTLE.  No, nor your holy vizard, to winne widdowes
  To give you legacies; or make zealous wives                    70
  To rob their husbands, for the *common cause*:
  Nor take the start of bonds, broke but one day,
  And say, *they were forfeited, by providence.*
  Nor shall you need, ore-night to eate huge meales,
  To celebrate your next daies fast the better:                    75
  The whilst the *Brethren*, and the *Sisters*, humbled,
  Abate the stiffenesse of the flesh. Nor cast
  Before your hungrie hearers, scrupulous bones,
  As whether a *Christian* may hawke, or hunt;

III. II. 46. Withall] F2, H.S.; With all Q, F.

Or whether, *Matrons, of the holy assembly*,                    80
May lay their haire out, or weare doublets:
Or have that idoll *Starch*, about their linnen.

ANANIAS.  It is, indeed, an idoll.

TRIBULATION.                    Mind him not, sir.
I doe command thee, spirit (of zeale, but trouble)
To peace within him. Pray you, sir, goe on.                    85

SUBTLE.  Nor shall you need to libell 'gainst the *Prelates*,
And shorten so your eares, against the hearing
Of the next wire-drawne grace. Nor, of necessitie,
Raile against playes, to please the *Alderman*,
Whose daily custard you devoure. Nor lie                    90
With zealous rage, till you are hoarse. Not one
Of these so singular arts. Nor call your selves,
By names of TRIBULATION, PERSECUTION,
RESTRAINT, LONG-PATIENCE, and such like, affected
By the whole family, or wood of you,                    95
Onely for glorie, and to catch the eare
Of the *Disciple*.

TRIBULATION.  Truely, sir, they are
Wayes, that the *godly Brethren* have invented,
For propagation of the *glorious cause*,
As very notable meanes, and whereby, also,                    100
Themselves grow soone, and profitably famous.

SUBTLE.  O, but the *stone*, all's idle to'it! nothing!
The art of *Angels*, Natures miracle,
The *divine secret*, that doth flye in clouds,
From *east* to *west*: and whose tradition                    105
Is not from men, but spirits.

ANANIAS.                    I hate *Traditions*:
I do not trust them—

TRIBULATION.                    Peace.

ANANIAS.                              They are *Popish*, all.
I will not peace. I will not—

TRIBULATION.                    ANANIAS.

ANANIAS.  Please the prophane, to grieve the godly: I may not.

SUBTLE.  Well, ANANIAS, thou shalt over-come.                    110

TRIBULATION.  It is an ignorant zeale, that haunts him, sir.

But truely, else, a very faithfull *Brother*,
A botcher: and a man, by revelation,
That hath a competent knowledge of the truth.

SUBTLE. Has he a competent summe, there, i'the bagg,        115
To buy the goods, within? I am made guardian,
And must, for charitie, and conscience sake,
Now, see the most be made, for my poore orphane:
Though I desire the *Brethren*, too, good gayners.
There they are, within. When you have view'd, and bought'hem,    120
And tane the inventorie of what they are,
They'are readie for *projection*; there's no more
To doe: cast on the *med'cine*, so much silver
As there is tinne there, so much gold as brasse,
I'll gi'it you in, by waight.

TRIBULATION.                But how long time,        125
Sir, must the *Saints* expect, yet?

SUBTLE.                Let me see,
How's the moone, now? Eight, nine, ten dayes hence
He will be *silver potate*; then three dayes,
Before he *citronise*: some fifteene dayes,
The *Magisterium* will be perfected.        130

ANANIAS. About the second day, of the third weeke,
In the ninth month?

SUBTLE.        Yes, my good ANANIAS.

TRIBULATION. What will the orphanes goods arise to, thinke
you?

SUBTLE. Some hundred markes; as much as fill'd three carres,
Unladed now: you'll make six millions of'hem.        135
But I must ha'more coales laid in.

TRIBULATION.                How!

SUBTLE.                Another load,
And then we ha' finish'd. We must now encrease
Our fire to *ignis ardens*, we are past
*Fimus equinus, Balnei, Cineris*,
And all those lenter heats. If the holy purse        140
Should, with this draught, fall low, and that the *Saints*
Doe need a present summe, I have a trick
To melt the pewter, you shall buy now, instantly,

142. a trick] F2, H.S.; trick Q, F.

And, with a tincture, make you as good *Dutch* dollers,
As any are in *Holland*.
TRIBULATION.                    Can you so?                    145
SUBTLE.   I, and shall bide the third examination.
ANANIAS.   It will be joyfull tidings to the *Brethren*.
SUBTLE.   But you must carry it, secret.
TRIBULATION.                                   I, but stay,
This act of coyning, is it lawfull?
ANANIAS.                         Lawfull?
We know no Magistrate. Or, if we did,                    150
This's forraine coyne.
SUBTLE.                    It is no coyning, sir.
It is but casting.
TRIBULATION.   Ha? you distinguish well.
Casting of money may be lawfull.
ANANIAS.                         'Tis, sir.
TRIBULATION.   Truely, I take it so.
SUBTLE.                         There is no scruple,
Sir, to be made of it; beleeve ANANIAS:                    155
This case of conscience he is studied in.
TRIBULATION.   I'll make a question of it, to the *Brethren*.
ANANIAS.   The *Brethren* shall approve it lawfull, doubt not.
Where shall't be done?
SUBTLE.                    For that wee'll talke, anone.

                                   *Knock without.*

There's some to speake with me. Goe in, I pray you,                    160
And view the parcells. That's the inventorie.
I'll come to you straight.

                    *Exeunt* ANANIAS *and* TRIBULATION.

                    Who is it? FACE! Appeare.


                    SCENE III

                    *Enter* FACE.

SUBTLE.   How now? Good prise?
FACE.                    Good poxe! Yond'caustive cheater
Never came on.

SUBTLE.          How then?

FACE.                    I ha'walk'd the round,
  Till now, and no such thing.

SUBTLE.                    And ha'you quit him?

FACE.  Quit him? and hell would quit him too, he were happy.
  'Slight would you have me stalke like a mill-jade,          5
  All day, for one, that will not yeeld us graines?
  I know him of old.

SUBTLE.                O, but to ha'gull'd him,
  Had beene a maistry.

FACE.                    Let him goe, black Boy,
  And turne thee, that some fresh newes may possesse thee.
  A noble *Count*, a *Don* of *Spaine* (my deare          10
  Delicious compeere, and my partie-bawd)
  Who is come hether, private, for his conscience,
  And brought munition with him, sixe great slopps,
  Bigger then three *Dutch* hoighs, beside round trunkes,
  Furnish'd with pistolets, and pieces of eight,          15
  Will straight be here, my rogue, to have thy bath
  (That is the colour,) and to make his battry
  Upon our DOL, our Castle, our *cinque*-Port,
  Our *Dover* pire, our what thou wilt. Where is shee?
  Shee must prepare perfumes, delicate linnen,          20
  The bath in chiefe, a banquet, and her wit,
  For shee must milke his *Epididimis*.
  Where is the *Doxie*?

SUBTLE.                I'll send her to thee:
  And but dispatch my brace of little JOHN LEYDENS,
  And come againe my selfe.

FACE.                    Are they within then?          25

SUBTLE.  Numbring the summe.

FACE.                How much?

SUBTLE.                        A hundred marks, Boy.

                              *Exit* SUBTLE.


FACE.  Why, this's a lucky day! Ten pounds of MAMMON!
  Three o'my clarke! A portague o'my grocer!
  This o'the *Brethren*! beside reversions,

And states, to come i'the widdow, and my *Count*! 　　30
My share, to day, will not be bought for fortie—

*Enter* DOL.

DOL.　　　　　　　　　　　　　　　　　　　What?
FACE. Pounds, daintie DOROTHEE, art thou so neere?
DOL. Yes, say lord *Generall*, how fares our campe?
FACE. As, with the few, that had entrench'd themselves
　　Safe, by their discipline, against a world, DOL:　　35
　　And laugh'd, within those trenches, and grew fat
　　With thinking on the booties, DOL, brought in
　　Daily, by their smali parties. This deare houre,
　　A doughtie *Don* is taken, with my DOL;
　　And thou maist make his ransome, what thou wilt,　　40
　　My *Dousabell*: He shall be brought here, fetter'd
　　With thy faire lookes, before he sees thee; and throwne
　　In a downe-bed, as darke as any dungeon;
　　Where thou shalt keepe him waking, with thy drum;
　　Thy drum, my DOL; thy drum; till he be tame　　45
　　As the poore black-birds were i'the great frost,
　　Or bees are with a bason: and so hive him
　　I'the swan-skin coverlid, and cambrick sheets,
　　Till he worke honey, and waxe, my little *Gods-guift*.
DOL. What is he, Generall?
FACE.　　　　　　　　　　　An *Adalantado*,　　50
　　A *Grande*, girle. Was not my DAPPER here, yet?
DOL. No.
FACE.　　　　Nor my DRUGGER?
DOL.　　　　　　　　　　　　Neither.
FACE.　　　　　　　　　　　　　　A poxe on'hem,
　　They are so long a furnishing! Such stinkards
　　Would not be seene, upon these festivall dayes.

*Enter* SUBTLE.

　　How now! ha'you done?
SUBTLE.　　　　　　　Done. They are gone. The summe　　55
　　Is here in banque, my FACE. I would, we knew
　　Another chapman, now, would buy'hem out-right.
FACE. 'Slid, NAB shall doo't, against he ha' the widdow,
　　To furnish houshold.

SUBTLE.                         Excellent, well thought on,
  Pray god, he come.
FACE.                         I pray, he keepe away                    60
  Till our new businesse be o're-past.
SUBTLE.                              But, FACE,
  How cam'st thou, by this secret *Don?*
FACE.                              A spirit
  Brought me th'intelligence, in a paper, here,
  As I was conjuring, yonder, in my circle
  For SURLY: I ha'my flies abroad. Your bath              65
  Is famous, SUBTLE, by my meanes. Sweet DOL,
  You must go tune your virginall, no loosing
  O'the least time. And, doe you heare? good action.
  Firke, like a flounder; kisse, like a scallop, close:
  And tickle him with thy mother-tongue. His great        70
  VERDUGO-ship has not a jot of language:
  So much the easier to be cossin'd, my DOLLY.
  He will come here, in a hir'd coach, obscure,
  And our owne coach-man, whom I have sent, as guide,
  No creature else.

>         *One knocks.* ⟨DOL *goes to the window.*⟩
>           Who's that?

SUBTLE.                         It i'not he?                    75
FACE.  O no, not yet this houre.
SUBTLE.                         Who is't?
DOL.                                   DAPPER,
  Your Clarke.
FACE.            Gods will, then, *Queene of Faerie,*
  On with your tyre; and, Doctor, with your robes.

>                  *Exit* DOL.

  Lett's dispatch him, for gods sake.
SUBTLE.                              'Twill be long.
FACE.  I warrant you, take but the *cues* I give you,         80
  It shall be briefe enough. ⟨*Goes to window.*⟩ 'Slight, here are
    more!
  ABEL, and I thinke, the angrie boy, the heire,
  That faine would quarrell.

     III. III. 59. Excellent,] F; ~ ₍ Q, *perhaps correctly.*
     66. famous,] H.S.; ~ ₍ Q, F.

SUBTLE.                    And the widdow?
FACE.                                               No,
  Not that I see. Away.

                                *Exit* SUBTLE.

⟨*To* DAPPER.⟩          O sir, you are welcome.


## SCENE IV

*Enter* DAPPER.

FACE.  The Doctor is within, a moving for you;
  (I have had the most adoe to winne him to it)
  He sweares, you'll be the dearling o'the dice:
  He never heard her *Highnesse* dote, till now (he sayes.)
  Your aunt has giv'n you the most gracious words,          5
  That can be thought on.
DAPPER.                    Shall I see her *Grace*?
FACE.  See her, and kisse her, too.

*Enter* DRUGGER *and* KASTRIL.

                            What? honest NAB!
  Ha'st brought the damaske?
DRUGGER.                    No, sir, here's *tabacco*.
FACE.  'Tis well done, NAB: Thou'lt bring the damaske too?
DRUGGER.  Yes, here's the gentleman, Captaine, master KASTRIL,          10
  I have brought to see the Doctor.
FACE.                                               Where's the widdow?
DRUGGER.  Sir, as he likes, his sister (he sayes) shall come.
FACE.  O, is it so? 'good time. Is your name KASTRIL, sir?
KASTRIL.  I, and the best o'the KASTRILS, I'lld be sorry else,
  By fifteene hundred, a yeere. Where is this Doctor?          15
  My mad *tabacco*-Boy, here, tells me of one,
  That can doe things. Has he any skill?
FACE.                                               Wherein, sir?
KASTRIL.  To carry a businesse, manage a quarrell, fairely,
  Upon fit termes.
FACE.                    It seemes sir, yo'are but yong
  About the towne, that can make that a question!          20
KASTRIL.  Sir, not so yong, but I have heard some speech
  Of the angrie Boyes, and seene'hem take *tabacco*;

And in his shop: and I can take it too.
And I would faine be one of'hem, and goe downe
And practise i'the countrey.
FACE.                    Sir, for the *Duello*,                    25
The Doctor, I assure you, shall informe you,
To the least shaddow of a haire: and shew you,
An instrument he has, of his owne making,
Where-with, no sooner shall you make report
Of any quarrell, but he will take the height on't,          30
Most instantly; and tell in what degree,
Of saf'ty it lies in, or mortalitie.
And, how it may be borne, whether in a *right line*,
Or a *halfe-circle*; or may, else, be cast
Into an *angle blunt*, if not *acute*:                    35
All this he will demonstrate. And then, rules,
To give, and take the lie, by.
KASTRIL.                    How? to take it?
FACE.   Yes, in *oblique*, hee'll shew you; or in *circle*:
But never in *diameter*. The whole towne
Studie his *theoremes*, and dispute them, ordinarily,      40
At the eating *Academies*.
KASTRIL.                    But, do's he teach
Living, by the wits, too?
FACE.                    Any thing, what ever.
You cannot thinke that subtiltie, but he reades it.
He made me a Captaine. I was a stark pimpe,
Just o'your standing, 'fore I met with him:              45
It i'not two months since. I'll tell you his method.
First, he will enter you, at some ordinarie.
KASTRIL.   No, I'll not come there. You shall pardon me.
FACE.                              For why, sir?
KASTRIL.   There's gaming there, and tricks.
FACE.                              Why, would you be
A gallant, and not game?
KASTRIL.                    I, 'twill spend a man.          50
FACE.   Spend you? It will repaire you, when you are spent.
How doe they live by their wits, there, that have vented
Six times your fortunes?
KASTRIL.                    What, three thousand a yeere!

FACE.   I, fortie thousand.

KASTRIL.                    Are there such?

FACE.                                              I, sir.

 And gallants, yet. Here's a yong gentleman,                    55
 Is borne to nothing, fortie markes a yeere,
 Which I count nothing. H'is to be initiated,
 And have a *flye* o'the Doctor. He will winne you
 By unresistable lucke, within this fortnight,
 Inough to buy a *baronie*. They will set him                    60
 Upmost, at the Groome-porters, all the *Christmasse*!
 And, for the whole yeere through, at everie place,
 Where there is play, present him with the chaire;
 The best attendance, the best drinke, sometimes
 Two glasses of *canarie*, and pay nothing;                    65
 The purest linnen, and the sharpest knife,
 The partrich next his trencher: and, somewhere,
 The daintie bed, in private, with the daintie.
 You shall ha'your ordinaries bid for him,
 As play-houses for a poet; and the master                    70
 Pray him, aloud, to name what dish he affects,
 Which must be butterd shrimps: and those that drinke
 To no mouth else, will drinke to his, as being
 The goodly, *president* mouth of all the boord.

KASTRIL.   Doe you not gull one?

FACE.                                   'Od's my life! Do you thinke it?   75
 You shall have a cast commander, (can but get
 In credit with a glover, or a spurrier,
 For some two paire, of eithers ware, afore-hand)
 Will, by most swift posts, dealing with him,
 Arrive at competent meanes, to keep himselfe,                    80
 His punke, and naked boy, in excellent fashion.
 And be admir'd for't.

KASTRIL.                    Will the Doctor teach this?

FACE.   He will doe more, sir, when your land is gone,
 (As men of spirit hate to keepe earth long)
 In a vacation, when small monie is stirring,                    85
 And ordinaries suspended till the tearme,
 Hee'll shew a perspective, where on one side
 You shall behold the faces, and the persons

Of all sufficient yong heires, in towne,
Whose bonds are currant for commoditie;                              90
On th'other side, the marchants formes, and others,
That, without helpe of any second broker,
(Who would expect a share) will trust such parcels:
In the third square, the verie street, and signe
Where the commoditie dwels, and do's but wait              95
To be deliver'd, be it pepper, sope,
Hops, or tabacco, oat-meale, woad, or cheeses.
All which you may so handle, to enjoy,
To your owne use, and never stand oblig'd.

KASTRIL.   I'faith! Is he such a fellow?

FACE.                          Why, NAB here knowes him.   100
And then for making matches, for rich widdowes,
Yong gentlewomen, heyres, the fortunat'st man!
Hee's sent too, farre, and neere, all over *England*,
To have his counsell, and to know their fortunes.

KASTRIL.   Gods will, my suster shall see him.

FACE.                               I'll tell you, sir,   105
What he did tell me of NAB. It's a strange thing!
(By the way you must eate no cheese, NAB, it breeds melancholy:
And that same melancholy breeds wormes) but passe it,
He told me, honest NAB, here, was ne'er at taverne,
But once in's life!

DRUGGER.            Truth, and no more I was not.         110

FACE.   And, then he was so sick—

DRUGGER.                        Could he tell you that, too?

FACE.   How should I know it?

DRUGGER.                    In troth we had beene a shooting,
And had a piece of fat ram-mutton, to supper,
That lay so heavy o'my stomack—

FACE.                           And he has no head
To beare any wine; for, what with the noise o'the fiddlers,   115
And care of his shop, for he dares keepe no servants—

DRUGGER.   My head did so ake—

FACE.                          As he was faine to be brought home,
The Doctor told me. And then, a good old woman—

DRUGGER.   (Yes faith, shee dwells in *Sea-coale*-lane) did cure me,
With sodden ale, and pellitorie o'the wall:                120

Cost me but two pence. I had another sicknesse,
Was worse then that.

FACE.                    I, that was with the griefe
Thou took'st for being sess'd at eighteene pence,
For the water-worke.

DRUGGER.                    In truth, and it was like
T'have cost me almost my life.

FACE.                    Thy haire went off?                    125

DRUGGER.   Yes, sir, 'twas done for spight.

FACE.                    Nay, so sayes the Doctor.

KASTRIL.   Pray thee, *tabacco*-Boy, goe fetch my suster,
I'll see this learned Boy, before I goe:
And so shall shee.

FACE.                    Sir, he is busie now:
But, if you have a sister to fetch hether,                    130
Perhaps, your owne paines may command her sooner;
And he, by that time, will be free.

KASTRIL.                    I goe.

*Exit* KASTRIL.

FACE.   DRUGGER, shee's thine: the damaske.

*Exit* DRUGGER.

(SUBTLE, and I

Must wrastle for her.) Come on, master DAPPER.
You see, how I turne clients, here, away,                    135
To give your cause dispatch. Ha'you perform'd
The ceremonies were injoyn'd you?

DAPPER.                    Yes, o'the vinegar,
And the cleane shirt.

FACE.                    'Tis well: that shirt may doe you
More worship then you thinke. Your aunt's a fire
But that shee will not shew it, t'have a sight on you.                    140
Ha'you provided for her *Graces* servants?

DAPPER.   Yes, here are six-score EDWARD shillings.

FACE.                    Good.

DAPPER.   And an old HARRY's soveraigne.

FACE.                    Very good.

DAPPER.   And three JAMES shillings, and an ELIZABETH groat,
Just twentie nobles.

FACE.　　　　　　　　O, you are too just.　　　　　145
I would you had had the other noble in MARIES.
DAPPER. I have some PHILIP, and MARIES.
FACE.　　　　　　　　　　　　　　I, those same
Are best of all. Where are they? Harke, the Doctor.

### SCENE V

*Enter* SUBTLE, *disguisd like a Priest of Faery.*

SUBTLE. Is yet her *Graces* cossen come?
FACE.　　　　　　　　　　　　　He is come.
SUBTLE. And is he fasting?
FACE.　　　　　　Yes.
SUBTLE.　　　　　　　　　And hath cry'd *hum*?
FACE. Thrise, you must answer.
DAPPER.　　　　　　　　　　Thrise.
SUBTLE.　　　　　　　　　　　　And as oft *buʒ*?
FACE. If you have, say.
DAPPER.　　　　　　I have.
SUBTLE.　　　　　　　　　　Then, to her cuz,
Hoping, that he hath vinegard his senses,　　　　　5
As he was bid, the *Faery Queene* dispenses,
By me, this robe, the petticote of FORTUNE;
Which that he straight put on, shee doth importune.

⟨DAPPER *puts on robe.*⟩

And though to FORTUNE neere be her petticote,
Yet, neerer is her smock, the Queene doth note:　　　10
And, therefore, even of that a piece shee hath sent,
Which, being a child, to wrap him in, was rent;
And prayes him, for a scarfe, he now will weare it
(With as much love, as then her *Grace* did teare it)
About his eyes, to shew, he is fortunate.　　　　　15

*They blind him with a rag.*

And, trusting unto her to make his state,
Hee'll throw away all worldly pelfe, about him;
Which that he will performe, shee doth not doubt him.
FACE. Shee need not doubt him, sir. Alas, he has nothing,
But what he will part withall, as willingly,　　　　20

Upon her *Graces* word (throw away your purse)
As shee would aske it: (hand-kerchiefes, and all)
Shee cannot bid that thing, but hee'll obay.
(If you have a ring, about you, cast it off,
Or a silver seale, at your wrist, her *Grace* will send        25
Her *Faeries* here to search you, therefore deale
Directly with her *Highnesse*.

                        *He throwes away, as they bid him.*
                        If they find
That you conceale a mite, you are un-done.)
DAPPER.  Truely, there's all.
FACE.                        All what?
DAPPER.                                My money, truly.
FACE.  Keepe nothing, that is transitorie, about you.        30
  (Bid DOL play musique.)

DOL *enters with a citterne: they pinch him.*

                        Looke, the *Elves* are come
To pinch you, if you tell not truth. Advise you.
DAPPER.  O, I have a paper with a spur-ryall in't.
FACE.                                *Ti, ti,*
  They knew't, they say.
SUBTLE.                *Ti, ti, ti, ti,* he has more yet.
FACE.  *Ti, ti-ti-ti.*  I'the tother pocket?
SUBTLE.                        *Titi, titi, titi, titi.*        35
  They must pinch him, or he will never confesse, they say.
DAPPER.  O, ô.
FACE.                Nay, 'pray you hold. He is her *Graces* nephew.
  *Ti, ti, ti?* What care you? Good faith, you shall care.
  Deale plainely, sir, and shame the *Faeries*. Shew
  You are an innocent.
DAPPER.                By this good light, I ha'nothing.        40
SUBTLE.  *Ti ti, ti ti to ta.* He do's equivocate, shee sayes:
  *Ti, ti do ti, ti ti do, ti da.* And sweares by the light, when he is
    blinded.
DAPPER.  By this good darke, I ha'nothing but a halfe-crowne
  Of gold, about my wrist, that my love gave me;
  And a leaden heart I wore, sin'shee forsooke me.        45

FACE.  I thought, 'twas something. And, would you incurre
    Your aunts displeasure for these trifles? Come,
    I had rather you had throwne away twentie halfe-crownes.
    You may weare your leaden heart still. How now?

⟨DOL *goes to the window.*⟩

SUBTLE.  What newes, DOL?

DOL.           Yonder's your knight, sir MAMMON.    50

FACE.  Gods lid, we never thought of him, till now.
    Where is he?

DOL.        Here, hard by. H'is at the doore.

SUBTLE.  And, you are not readie, now? DOL, get his suit.

*Exit* DOL.

    He must not be sent back.

FACE.        O, by no meanes.
    What shall we doe with this same Puffin, here,    55
    Now hee's o'the spit?

SUBTLE.      Why, lay him back a while,
    With some device. *Ti, ti ti, ti ti ti.* Would her *Grace* speake with
      me?
    I come.

*Enter* DOL, ⟨*with* FACE'S *alchemical costume.*⟩

        Helpe, DOL.

FACE.         Who's there? Sir EPICURE;

*He speaks through the key-hole, the other
knocking.* ⟨DOL *helps to dress him.*⟩

    My master's i'the way. Please you to walke
    Three or foure turnes, but till his back be turn'd,    60
    And I am for you. Quickly, DOL.

SUBTLE.        Her *Grace*
    Commends her kindly to you, master DAPPER.

DAPPER.  I long to see her *Grace.*

SUBTLE.        Shee, now, is set
    At dinner, in her bed; and shee has sent you,
    From her owne private trencher, a dead mouse,    65
    And a piece of ginger-bread, to be merry withall,
    And stay your stomack, lest you faint with fasting:

Yet, if you could hold out, till shee saw you (shee sayes)
It would be better for you.

FACE.                              Sir, he shall
Hold out, and 'twere this two houres, for her *Highnesse*;          70
I can assure you that. We will not loose
All we ha'done—

SUBTLE.                    He must nor see, nor speake
To any body, till then.

FACE.                              For that, wee'll put, sir,
A stay in'is mouth.

SUBTLE.                Of what?

FACE.                                    Of ginger-bread.
Make you it fit. He that hath pleas'd her *Grace*,          75
Thus farre, shall not now crinckle, for a little.
Gape sir, and let him fit you.

⟨*They gag him.*⟩

SUBTLE.                              Where shall we now
Bestow him?

DOL.            I'the privie.

SUBTLE.                              Come along, sir,
I now must shew you *Fortunes* privy lodgings.

FACE.  Are they perfum'd? and his bath readie?

SUBTLE.                                    All.          80
Onely the Fumigation's somewhat strong.

FACE.  Sir EPICURE, I am yours, sir, by and by.

*Exeunt.*


# ACT IV

## SCENE I

### *Enter* FACE *and* MAMMON.

FACE.  O, sir, yo'are come i'the onely, finest time—

MAMMON.  Where's master?

FACE.                              Now preparing for projection, sir.
Your stuffe will b'all chang'd shortly.

MAMMON.                                    Into gold?

FACE.  To gold, and silver, sir.

MAMMON.                          Silver, I care not for.
FACE.  Yes, sir, a little to give beggars.
MAMMON.                              Where's the lady?        5
FACE.  At hand, here. I ha'told her such brave things, o'you,
  Touching your bountie and your noble spirit—
MAMMON.                                    Hast thou?
FACE.  As shee is almost in her fit to see you.
  But, good sir, no *divinitie* i'your conference,
  For feare of putting her in rage—
MAMMON.                          I warrant thee.             10
FACE.  Sixe men will not hold her downe. And, then
  If the old man should heare, or see you—
MAMMON.                              Feare not.
FACE.  The very house, sir, would runne mad. You know it
  How scrupulous he is, and violent,
  'Gainst the least act of sinne. *Physick*, or *Mathematiques*,   15
  *Poetrie*, *State*, or *Bawdry* (as I told you)
  Shee will endure, and never startle: But
  No word of controversie.
MAMMON.                      I am school'd, good Ulen.
FACE.  And you must praise her house, remember that,
  And her nobilitie.
MAMMON.          Let me alone:                                20
  No *Herald*, no nor *Antiquarie*, *Lungs*,
  Shall doe it better. Goe.
FACE.  ⟨*Aside.*⟩            Why, this is yet
  A kind of moderne happinesse, to have
  DOL Common for a great lady.

                                        *Exit* FACE.


MAMMON.                      Now, EPICURE,
  Heighten thy selfe, talke to her, all in gold;               25
  Raine her as many showers, as JOVE did drops
  Unto his DANAE: Shew the *God* a miser,
  Compar'd with MAMMON. What? the *stone* will do't.
  Shee shall feele gold, tast gold, heare gold, sleepe gold:
  Nay, we will *concumbere* gold. I will be puissant,          30
  And mightie in my talke to her! Here shee comes.

              IV. I. 20. me‸]  ∼, Q, F, H.S.

*Enter* FACE *and* DOL.

FACE.  To him, DOL, suckle him. This is the noble knight,
  I told your ladiship—
MAMMON.                    Madame, with your pardon,
  I kisse your vesture.
DOL.                    Sir, I were un-civill
  If I would suffer that, my lip to you, sir.                    35
MAMMON.  I hope, my lord your brother be in health, lady?
DOL.  My lord, my brother is, though I no ladie, sir.
FACE.  (Well said my *Guiny*-bird.)
MAMMON.                    Right noble madame—
FACE.  (O, we shall have most fierce idolatrie!)
MAMMON.  'Tis your prerogative.
DOL.                    Rather your courtesie.                    40
MAMMON.  Were there nought else t'inlarge your vertues, to me,
  These answeres speake your breeding, and your bloud.
DOL.  Bloud we boast none, sir, a poore Baron's daughter.
MAMMON.  Poore! and gat you? Prophane not. Had your father
  Slept all the happy remnant of his life                    45
  After that act, lyen but there still, and panted,
  H'had done inough, to make himselfe, his issue,
  And his posteritie noble.
DOL.                    Sir, although
  We may be said to want the guilt, and trappings,
  The dresse of honor; yet we strive to keepe                    50
  The seedes, and the materialls.
MAMMON.                    I doe see
  The old ingredient, vertue, was not lost,
  Nor the drug, money, us'd to make your compound.
  There is a strange nobilitie, i'your eye,
  This lip, that chin! Me thinks you doe resemble                    55
  One o'the *Austriack* princes.
FACE. ⟨*Aside.*⟩                    Very like,
  Her father was an *Irish* costar-monger.
MAMMON.  The house of *Valois*, just, had such a nose.
  And such a fore-head, yet, the *Medici*
  Of *Florence* boast.

53. drug,] H.S.; ∼ ₍ F; *Drug,* Q.

DOL.                    Troth, and I have beene lik'ned          60
  To all these Princes.
FACE. ⟨*Aside.*⟩          I'll be sworne, I heard it.
MAMMON.  I know not how! it is not any one,
  But ee'n the very choise of all their features.
FACE. ⟨*Aside.*⟩  I'll in, and laugh.

                                              *Exit* FACE.

MAMMON.                    A certaine touch, or aire,
  That sparkles a divinitie, beyond          65
  An earthly beautie!
DOL.                    O, you play the courtier.
MAMMON.  Good lady, gi'me leave—
DOL.                    In faith, I may not,
  To mock me, sir.
MAMMON.          To burne i'this sweet flame:
  The *Phœnix* never knew a nobler death.
DOL.  Nay, now you court the courtier: and destroy          70
  What you would build. This art, sir, i'your words,
  Calls your whole faith in question.
MAMMON.                    By my soule—
DOL.  Nay, oathes are made o'the same aire, sir.
MAMMON.                              Nature
  Never bestow'd upon mortalitie,
  A more unblam'd, a more harmonious feature:          75
  Shee play'd the step-dame in all faces, else.
  Sweet madame, le'me be particular—
DOL.  Particular, sir? I pray you, know your distance.
MAMMON.  In no ill sense, sweet ladie, but to aske
  How your fair graces passe the houres? I see          80
  Yo'are lodg'd, here, i'the house of a rare man,
  An excellent Artist: but, what's that to you?
DOL.  Yes, sir. I studie here the *mathematiques*,
  And distillation.
MAMMON.          O, I crie your pardon.
  H'is a divine instructer! can extract          85
  The soules of all things, by his art; call all
  The vertues, and the miracles of the Sunne,
  Into a temperate fornace: teach dull nature

What her owne forces are. A man, the Emp'rour
Has courted, above KELLEY: sent his medalls,　　　　　90
And chaines, t'invite him.

DOL.　　　　　　　　I, and for his physick, sir—

MAMMON.  Above the art of ÆSCULAPIUS,
That drew the envy of the Thunderer!
I know all this, and more.

DOL.　　　　　　　　Troth, I am taken, sir,
Whole, with these studies, that contemplate nature.　　　95

MAMMON.  It is a noble humour. But, this forme
Was not intended to so darke a use!
Had you beene crooked, foule, of some course mould,
A cloyster had done well: but, such a feature
That might stand up the glorie of a kingdome,　　　100
To live recluse! is a mere *solæcisme*,
Though in a nunnery. It must not be.
I muse, my lord your brother will permit it!
You should spend halfe my land first, were I hee.
Do's not this diamant better, on my finger,　　　105
Then i'the quarrie?

DOL.　　　　　Yes.

MAMMON.　　　　　　Why, you are like it.
You were created, lady, for the light!
Heare, you shall weare it; take it, the first pledge
Of what I speake: to binde you, to beleeve me.

DOL.  In chaines of adamant?

MAMMON.　　　　　　Yes, the strongest bands.　　　110
And take a secret, too. Here, by your side,
Doth stand, this houre, the happiest man, in *Europe*.

DOL.  You are contented, sir?

MAMMON.　　　　　　Nay, in true being:
The envy of Princes, and the feare of States.

DOL.  Say you so, sir EPICURE!

MAMMON.　　　　　　Yes, and thou shalt prove it,　　　115
Daughter of honor. I have cast mine eye
Upon thy forme, and I will reare this beautie,
Above all stiles.

DOL.　　　　You meane no treason, sir!

MAMMON.  No, I will take away that jealousie.

I am the lord of the *Philosophers stone*,                    120
And thou the lady.

DOL.                        How sir! ha'you that?

MAMMON.   I am the master of the *maistrie*.
This day, the good old wretch, here, o'the house
Has made it for us. Now, hee's at *projection*.
Thinke therefore, thy first wish, now; let me heare it:      125
And it shall raine into thy lap, no shower,
But flouds of gold, whole cataracts, a deluge,
To get a nation on thee!

DOL.                        You are pleas'd, sir,
To worke on the ambition of our sexe.

MAMMON.   I'am pleas'd, the glorie of her sexe should know,   130
This nooke, here, of the *Friers*, is no climate
For her, to live obscurely in, to learne
Physick, and surgery, for the Constables wife
Of some odde Hundred in *Essex*; but come forth,
And tast the aire of palaces; eate, drinke                   135
The toyles of *Emp'ricks*, and their boasted practice;
Tincture of pearle, and corrall, gold, and amber;
Be seene at feasts, and triumphs; have it ask'd,
What miracle shee is? set all the eyes
Of court a-fire, like a burning glasse,                      140
And worke'hem into cinders; when the jewells
Of twentie states adorne thee; and the light
Strikes out the starres; that, when thy name is mention'd,
Queenes may looke pale: and, we but shewing our love,
NERO'S POPPÆA may be lost in storie!                          145
Thus, will we have it.

DOL.                        I could well consent, sir.
But, in a monarchy, how will this be?
The Prince will soone take notice; and both seize
You, and your *stone*: it being a wealth unfit
For any private subject.

MAMMON.                        If he knew it.                 150

DOL.  Your selfe doe boast it, sir.

MAMMON.                        To thee, my life.

DOL.  O, but beware, sir! You may come to end

The remnant of your daies, in a loth'd prison,
By speaking of it.
MAMMON.                    'Tis no idle feare!
Wee'll therefore goe with all, my girle, and live                    155
In a free state; where we will eate our mullets,
Sous'd in high-countrey wines, sup phesants egges,
And have our cockles, boild in silver shells,
Our shrimps to swim againe, as when they liv'd,
In a rare butter, made of dolphins milke,                    160
Whose creame do's looke like opalls: and, with these
Delicate meats, set our selves high for pleasure,
And take us downe againe, and then renew
Our youth, and strength, with drinking the *elixir*,
And so enjoy a perpetuitie                    165
Of life, and lust. And, thou shalt ha'thy wardrobe,
Richer then *Natures*, still, to change thy selfe,
And vary oftner, for thy pride, then shee:
Or *Art*, her wise, and almost-equall servant.

*Enter* FACE.

FACE.  Sir, you are too loud. I heare you, every word,                    170
Into the laboratory. Some fitter place.
The garden, or great chamber above. How like you her?
MAMMON.  Excellent! *Lungs*.  There's for thee.

⟨*Gives him money.*⟩

FACE.                                        But, doe you heare?
Good sir, beware, no mention of the *Rabbines*.
MAMMON.  We thinke not on'hem.
FACE.                                        O, it is well, sir.

*Exeunt* MAMMON *and* DOL.

SUBTLE!  175


SCENE II

*Enter* SUBTLE.

FACE.  Dost thou not laugh?
SUBTLE.                                        Yes. Are they gone?
FACE.                                                            All's cleare.
          D

SUBTLE.   The widdow is come.

FACE.                                        And your quarrelling disciple?

SUBTLE.   I

FACE.            I must to my Captaine-ship againe, then.

SUBTLE.   Stay, bring'hem in, first.

FACE.                                         So I meant. What is shee?
   A *Bony-bell?*

SUBTLE.            I know not.

FACE.                                    Wee'll draw lots,                    5
   You'll stand to that?

SUBTLE.              What else?

FACE.                                    O, for a suite,
   To fall now, like a cortine: flap.

SUBTLE.                         To th'dore, man.

FACE.   You'll ha'the first kisse, 'cause I am not readie.

SUBTLE.   ⟨*Aside.*⟩ Yes, and perhaps hit you through both the
                                         nostrils.

FACE.   ⟨*At door.*⟩ Who would you speak with?

KASTRIL.   ⟨*Within.*⟩                        Wher's the Captaine?

FACE.                                           Gone, sir,   10
   About some businesse.

KASTRIL.              Gone?

FACE.                                    Hee'll returne straight.
   But master Doctor, his Lieutenant, is here.

*Exit* FACE.

*Enter* KASTRIL *and* DAME PLIANT.

SUBTLE.   Come neere, my worshipfull Boy, my *terræ Fili,*
   That is, my Boy of land; make thy approches:
   Welcome, I know thy lusts, and thy desires,                    15
   And I will serve, and satisfie'hem. Beginne,
   Charge me from thence, or thence, or in this line;
   Here is my center: Ground thy quarrell.

KASTRIL.                                    You lie.

SUBTLE.   How, child of wrath, and anger! the loud lie?
   For what, my sodaine Boy?

KASTRIL.                         Nay, that looke you too,                    20
   I am afore-hand.

SUBTLE.                    O, this's no true *Grammar*,
And as ill *Logick*! You must render causes, child,
Your first, and second *Intentions*, know your *canons*,
And your *divisions*, *moodes*, *degrees*, and *differences*,
Your *prædicaments*, *substance*, and *accident*,                    25
*Series externe*, and *interne*, with their *causes*
*Efficient*, *materiall*, *formall*, *finall*,
And ha'your *elements* perfect—

KASTRIL.                    What is this!
The angrie tongue he talkes in?

SUBTLE.                    That false precept,
Of being afore-hand, has deceiv'd a number;                    30
And made'hem enter quarrells, often-times,
Before they were aware: and, afterward,
Against their wills.

KASTRIL.          How must I doe then, sir?

SUBTLE.  I crie this lady mercy. Shee should, first,
Have beene saluted. I doe call you lady,                    35
Because you are to be one, ere't be long,
My soft, and buxome widdow.

                                        *He kisses her.*

KASTRIL.                    Is shee, i-faith?

SUBTLE.  Yes, or my art is an egregious lyar.

KASTRIL.  How know you?

SUBTLE.                    By inspection, on her fore-head,
And subtiltie of her lip, which must be tasted                    40
Often, to make a judgement.

                                   *He kisses her againe.*
                              'Slight, shee melts
Like a *Myrobalane*! Here is, yet, a line
In *rivo frontis*, tells me, he is no knight.

PLIANT.  What is he then, sir?

SUBTLE.                    Let me see your hand.
O, your *linea Fortunæ* makes it plaine;                    45
And *stella*, here, in *monte Veneris*:
But, most of all, *junctura annularis*.
He is a souldier, or a man of art, lady:
But shall have some great honour, shortly.

PLIANT.                                          Brother,
 Hee's a rare man, beleeve me!
KASTRIL.                          Hold your peace.                50

*Enter* FACE, ⟨*in his captain's costume.*⟩

 Here comes the tother rare man. 'Save you Captaine.
FACE.  Good master KASTRIL.  Is this your sister?
KASTRIL.                                          I, sir.
 Please you to kusse her, and be proud to know her?
FACE.  I shall be proud to know you, ladie.
PLIANT.                                          Brother,
 He calls me ladie, too.
KASTRIL.                     I, peace. I heard it.                55
FACE.  ⟨*To* SUBTLE.⟩ The *Count* is come.
SUBTLE.                          Where is he?
FACE.                                          At the dore.
SUBTLE.  Why, you must entertaine him.
FACE.                                     What'll you doe
 With these the while?
SUBTLE.                     Why, have'hem up, and shew'hem
 Some fustian booke, or the darke glasse.
FACE.                                     'Fore god,
 Shee is a delicate dab-chick! I must have her.            60
SUBTLE.  Must you? I, if your fortune will, you must.

                                        *Exit* FACE.

 Come sir, the Captaine will come to us presently.
 I'll ha'you to my chamber of *demonstrations*,
 Where I'll shew you both the *Grammar*, and *Logick*,
 And *Rhetorick* of quarrelling; my whole method,          65
 Drawne out in tables: and my instrument,
 That hath the severall scale upon't, shall make you
 Able to quarrell, at a strawes breadth, by *Moone*-light.
 And, lady, I'll have you looke in a glasse,
 Some halfe an houre, but to cleare your eye-sight,        70
 Against you see your fortune: which is greater,
 Then I may judge upon the sodaine, trust me.
                                        *Exeunt.*

### SCENE III

*Enter* FACE.

FACE.  Where are you, Doctor?
SUBTLE.  ⟨*Within.*⟩        I'll come to you presently.
FACE.  I will ha'this same widdow, now I ha'seene her,
    On any composition.

*Enter* SUBTLE.

SUBTLE.          What doe you say?
FACE.  Ha'you dispos'd of them?
SUBTLE.              I ha'sent'hem up.
FACE.  SUBTLE, in troth, I needs must have this widdow.        5
SUBTLE.  Is that the matter?
FACE.        Nay, but heare me.
SUBTLE.              Goe to,
    If you rebell once, DOL shall know it all.
    Therefore, be quiet, and obey your chance.
FACE.  Nay, thou art so violent now—Doe but conceive:
    Thou art old, and canst not serve—
SUBTLE.          Who, cannot I?        10
    'Slight, I will serve her with thee, for a—
FACE.          Nay,
    But understand: I'll gi'you composition.
SUBTLE.  I will not treat with thee: what, sell my fortune?
    'Tis better then my birth-right. Doe not murmure.
    Winne her, and carrie her. If you grumble, DOL        15
    Knowes it directly.
FACE.        Well sir, I am silent.
    Will you goe helpe, to fetch in *Don*, in state?
SUBTLE.  I follow you, sir:

                                *Exit* FACE.

                    we must keepe FACE in awe,
    Or he will over-looke us like a tyranne.

*Enter* FACE, *and* SURLY *like a Spaniard.*

    Braine of a taylor! Who comes here? *Don* JON!        20
SURLY.  ⟨*Bows.*⟩ *Sennores, beso las manos, à vuestras mercedes.*

SUBTLE.  Would you had stoup'd a little, and kist our *anos*.

FACE.  Peace SUBTLE.

SUBTLE.                    Stab me; I shall never hold, man.
  He lookes in that deepe ruffe, like a head in a platter,
  Serv'd in by a short cloake upon two tressils!          25

FACE.  Or, what doe you say to a collar of brawne, cut downe
  Beneath the souse, and wriggled with a knife?

SUBTLE.  'Slud, he do's looke too fat to be a *Spaniard*.

FACE.  Perhaps some *Fleming*, or some *Hollander* got him
  In D'ALVA's time: *Count* EGMONTS bastard.

SUBTLE.                              *Don*,          30
  Your scirvy, yellow, *Madrid* face is welcome.

SURLY.  *Gratia*.

SUBTLE.          He speakes, out of a fortification.
  'Pray god, he ha'no squibs in those deepe sets.

SURLY.  *Por dios, Sennores, muy linda casa!*

SUBTLE.  What sayes he?

FACE.                    Praises the house, I thinke,          35
  I know no more but's action.

SUBTLE.                    Yes, the *Casa*,
  My precious DIEGO, will prove faire inough,
  To cossen you in. Doe you marke? you shall
  Be cossened, DIEGO.

FACE.                    Cossened, doe you see?
  My worthy *Donƶel*, cossened.

SURLY.                    *Entiendo*.          40

SUBTLE.  Doe you intend it? So doe we, deare *Don*.
  Have you brought pistolets? or portagues?
  My solemne *Don*? Dost thou feele any?

                              *He feeles his pockets.*

FACE.                              Full.

SUBTLE.  You shall be emptied, *Don*; pumped, and drawne,
  Drie, as they say.

FACE.                    Milked, in troth, sweet *Don*.          45

SUBTLE.  See all the monsters; the great lyon of all, *Don*.

SURLY.  *Con licencia, se puede ver à esta Sennorà?*

SUBTLE.  What talkes he now?

FACE.                    O'the *Sennora*.

SUBTLE.                              O, *Don*,

That is the lyonesse, which you shall see
Also, my *Don*.

FACE.                    'Slid, SUBTLE, how shall we doe?                    50

SUBTLE.  For what?

FACE.                    Why, DOL's emploi'd, you know.

SUBTLE.                                        That's true!
'Fore heav'n I know not: He must stay, that's all.

FACE.  Stay? That he must not by no meanes.

SUBTLE.                                        No, why?

FACE.  Unlesse you'll marre all. 'Slight, hee'll suspect it.
And then he will not pay, not halfe so well.                    55
This is a travell'd punque-master, and do's know
All the delayes: a notable hot raskall,
And lookes, already, rampant.

SUBTLE.                    'Sdeath, and MAMMON
Must not be troubled.

FACE.                    MAMMON, in no case!

SUBTLE.  What shall we doe then?

FACE.                    Thinke: you must be sodaine.  60

SURLY.  *Entiendo, que la Sennora es tan hermosa, que condìcio tan
à ver la, como la bien aventuránça de mi vida.*

FACE.  *Mi vida?* 'Slid, SUBTLE, he puts me in minde o'the widow.
What dost thou say to draw her to't? ha?
And tell her, it is her fortune. All our venter                    65
Now lies upon't. It is but one man more,
Which on's chance to have her: and, beside,
There is no maiden-head, to be fear'd, or lost.
What dost thou thinke on't, SUBTLE?

SUBTLE.                    Who, I? Why—

FACE.  The credit of our house too is engag'd.                    70

SUBTLE.  You made me an offer for my share e're while.
What wilt thou gi'me, i-faith?

FACE.                    O, by that light,
Ile not buy now. You know your doome to me.
E'en take your lot, obey your chance, sir; winne her,
And weare her, out for me.

SUBTLE.                    'Slight. I'll not worke her then.  75

FACE.  It is the common cause, therefore bethinke you.
DOL else must know it, as you said.

SUBTLE.　　　　　　　　　　　　　　I care not.

SURLY.　*Sennores, por que se tarda tanta?*

SUBTLE.　Faith, I am not fit, I am old.

FACE.　　　　　　　　　　That's now no reason, sir.

SURLY.　*Puede ser, de ha*$z$*er burla de mi amor.*　　　　　　8o

FACE.　You heare the *Don*, too? By this ayre, I call,
　And loose the hinges. DOL.

SUBTLE.　　　　　　　　　A plague of hell—

FACE.　Will you then doe?

SUBTLE.　　　　　　　　Yo'are a terrible rogue,
　Ile thinke of this: will you, sir, call the widow?

FACE.　Yes, and Ile take her too, with all her faults,　　85
　Now I doe thinke on't better.

SUBTLE.　　　　　　　　With all my heart, sir,
　Am I discharg'd o'the lot?

FACE.　　　　　　　　As you please.

SUBTLE.　　　　　　　　　　　Hands.

FACE.　Remember now, that upon any change,
　You never claime her.

SUBTLE.　　　　　　　Much good joy, and health to you, sir.
　Marry a whore? *Fate*, let me wed a witch first.　　　90

SURLY.　*Por estas honrada's barbas—*

SUBTLE.　　　　　　　　　He sweares by his beard.
　Dispatch, and call the brother too.

　　　　　　　　　　　　　　　　*Exit* FACE.

SURLY.　　　　　　　　*Tiengo dùda, Sennores,*
　*Que no me hágan alguna traycion.*

SUBTLE.　How, issue on? Yes, *præsto Sennor*. Please you
　*Enthratha* the *chambratha*, worthy *Don*;　　　　　95
　Where if it please the *Fates*, in your *bathada*,
　You shall be sok'd, and strok'd, and tub'd, and rub'd:
　And scrub'd, and fub'd, deare *Don*, before you goe.
　You shall, in faith, my scirvie babioun *Don*:
　Be curried, claw'd, and flaw'd, and taw'd, indeed.　　1oo
　I will the heartilier goe about it now,
　And make the widdow a punke, so much the sooner,
　To be reveng'd on this impetuous FACE:
　The quickly doing of it is the grace.

　　　　　　　　　　　　　　　　*Exeunt.*

SCENE IV

*Enter* FACE, KASTRIL *and* DAME PLIANT.

FACE.   Come ladie: I knew, the Doctor would not leave,
  Till he had found the very nick of her fortune.
KASTRIL.   To be a *Countesse*, say you?
FACE.                          A *Spanish Countesse*, sir.
PLIANT.   Why? is that better then an *English Countesse?*
FACE.   Better? 'Slight, make you that a question, ladie?            5
KASTRIL.   Nay, shee is a foole, Captaine, you must pardon her.
FACE.   Aske from your courtier, to your innes of court-man,
  To your mere millaner: they will tell you all,
  Your *Spanish* jennet is the best horse. Your *Spanish*
  Stoupe is the best garbe. Your *Spanish* beard              10
  Is the best cut. Your *Spanish* ruffes are the best
  Weare. Your *Spanish Pavin* the best daunce.
  Your *Spanish* titillation in a glove
  The best perfume. And, for your *Spanish* pike,
  And *Spanish* blade, let your poore Captaine speake.            15

*Enter* SUBTLE.

  Here comes the Doctor.
SUBTLE.                    My most honor'd ladie,
  (For so I am now to stile you, having found
  By this my *scheme*, you are to under-goe
  An honorable fortune, very shortly.)
  What will you say now, if some—
FACE.                          I ha'told her all, sir.           20
  And her right worshipfull brother, here, that shee shall be
  A *Countesse*: doe not delay'hem, sir. A *Spanish Countesse.*
SUBTLE.   Still, my scarse worshipfull Captaine, you can keepe
  No secret. Well, since he has told you, madame,
  Doe you forgive him, and I doe.
KASTRIL.                    Shee shall doe that, sir.          25
  I'le looke to't, 'tis my charge.
SUBTLE.                    Well then. Nought rests
  But that shee fit her love, now, to her fortune.

PLIANT.   Truely, I shall never brooke a *Spaniard*.

SUBTLE.                                         No?

PLIANT.   Never, sin'*eighty-eight* could I abide'hem,
    And that was some three yeere afore I was borne, in truth.     30

SUBTLE.  Come, you must love him, or be miserable:
    Choose, which you will.

FACE.                      By this good rush, perswade her,
    Shee will crie straw-berries else, within this twelve-month.

SUBTLE.   Nay, shads, and mackrell, which is worse.

FACE.                                         Indeed, sir?

KASTRIL.   Gods lid, you shall love him, or Ile kick you.

PLIANT.                                         Why?   35
    Ile doe as you will ha'me, brother.

KASTRIL.                      Doe,
    Or by this hand, I'll maull you.

FACE.                      Nay, good sir,
    Be not so fierce.

SUBTLE.             No, my enraged child,
    Shee will be rul'd. What, when she comes to tast
    The pleasures of a Countesse! to be courted—     40

FACE.   And kist, and ruffled!

SUBTLE.                      I, behind the hangings.

FACE.   And then come forth in pomp!

SUBTLE.                         And know her state!

FACE.   Of keeping all th'idolaters o'the chamber
    Barer to her, then at their prayers!

SUBTLE.                   Is serv'd
    Upon the knee!

FACE.             And has her pages, huishers,     45
    Foot-men, and coaches—

SUBTLE.                Her six mares—

FACE.                         Nay, eight!

SUBTLE.   To hurry her through *London*, to th'*Exchange*,
    *Bet'lem*, the *China*-houses—

FACE.                      Yes, and have
    The citizens gape at her, and praise her tyres!
    And my-lords goose-turd bands, that rides with her!     50

KASTRIL.   Most brave! By this hand, you are not my suster
    If you refuse.

PLIANT.            I will not refuse, brother.

*Enter* SURLY.

SURLY.  *Que es esto, Sennores, que non se venga?*
  *Esta tardança me mata!*

FACE.                  It is the *Count* come!
  The Doctor knew he would be here, by his art.                    55

SUBTLE.  *En gallanta Madama, Don! gallantissima!*

SURLY.  *Por tódos los dioses, la mas acabada*
  *Hermosura, que he visto en mi vìda.*

FACE.  Is't not a gallant language, that they speake?

KASTRIL.  An admirable language! Is't not *French?*                60

FACE.  No, *Spanish*, sir.

KASTRIL.              It goes like law-*French*,
  And that, they say, is the court-liest language.

FACE.                              List, sir.

SURLY.  *El Sol ha perdido su lumbre, con el*
  *Resplandor, que tràe esta dama. Valga me dios!*

FACE.  He'admires your sister.

KASTRIL.              Must not shee make curtsie?                  65

SUBTLE.  'Ods will, shee must goe to him, man; and kisse him!
  It is the *Spanish* fashion, for the women
  To make first court.

FACE.            'Tis true he tells you, sir:
  His art knowes all.

SURLY.              *Por que no se acùde?*

KASTRIL.  He speakes to her, I thinke?

FACE.                      That he do's sir.                        70

SURLY.  *Por el amor de dios, que es esto, que se tàrda?*

KASTRIL.  Nay, see: shee will not understand him! Gull.
  Noddy.

PLIANT.  What say you brother?

KASTRIL.                  Asse, my suster,
  Goe kusse him, as the cunning man would ha'you,
  I'll thrust a pinne i'your buttocks else.

FACE.                          O, no sir.                          75

SURLY.  *Sennora mia, mi persona muy indigna esta*
  *A llegar à tànta Hermosura.*

                              ⟨*They kiss.*⟩

FACE.  Do's he not use her bravely?

KASTRIL.                              Bravely, i-faith!

FACE.  Nay, he will use her better.

KASTRIL.                              Doe you thinke so?

SURLY.  *Sennora, si sera servida, entremus.*                              80

                              *Exeunt* SURLY *and* PLIANT.

KASTRIL.  Where do's he carry her?

FACE.                              Into the garden, sir;
   Take you no thought: I must interpret for her.

SUBTLE.  ⟨*To* FACE.⟩ Give DOL the word.

                              *Exit* FACE.
                    Come, my fierce child, advance,
   Wee'll to our quarrelling lesson againe.

KASTRIL.                              Agreed.
   I love a *Spanish* Boy, with all my heart.                              85

SUBTLE.  Nay, and by this meanes, sir, you shall be brother
   To a great *Count.*

KASTRIL.          I, I knew that, at first.
   This match will advance the house of the KASTRILS.

SUBTLE.  'Pray god, your sister prove but pliant.

KASTRIL.                              Why,
   Her name is so: by her other husband.

SUBTLE.                              How!                              90

KASTRIL.  The widdow PLIANT. Knew you not that?

SUBTLE.                              No faith, sir.
   Yet, by erection of her *figure,* I gest it.
   Come, let's goe practice.

KASTRIL.          Yes, but doe you thinke, Doctor,
   I e'er shall quarrell well?

SUBTLE.                              I warrant you.

                              *Exeunt.*


SCENE V

*Enter* DOL, *in her fit of talking, and* MAMMON.

DOL.  For, *after* ALEXANDERS *death*—

MAMMON.                              Good lady—

DOL. *That* PERDICCAS, *and* ANTIGONUS *were slaine,*
　*The two that stood,* SELEUC', *and* PTOLOMEE—
MAMMON. Madame.
DOL. 　　　　　　　　*Made up the two legs, and the fourth Beast.*
　*That was Gog-north, and Egypt-south: which after*　　　5
　*Was call'd Gog Iron-leg, and South Iron-leg—*
MAMMON. 　　　　　　　　　　　　Lady—
DOL. *And then Gog-horned. So was Egypt, too.*
　*Then Egypt clay-leg, and Gog clay-leg—*
MAMMON. 　　　　　　　　Sweet madame.
DOL. *And last Gog-dust, and Egypt-dust, which fall*
　*In the last linke of the fourth chaine. And these*　　　10
　*Be starres in story, which none see, or looke at—*
MAMMON. What shall I doe?
DOL. 　　　　　　　*For, as he sayes, except*
　*We call the Rabbines, and the heathen Greekes—*
MAMMON. Deare lady.
DOL. 　　　　　　*To come from Salem, and from Athens,*
　*And teach the people of great Britaine—*

*Enter* FACE, ⟨*in his alchemical costume.*⟩

FACE. 　　　　　　　　　　What's the matter, sir?　15
DOL. *To speake the tongue of* EBER, *and* JAVAN—
MAMMON. 　　　　　　　　　　O,
　Sh'is in her fit.
DOL. 　　　　*We shall know nothing—*
FACE. 　　　　　　　　Death, sir,
　We are un-done.
DOL. 　　　*Where, then, a learned Linguist*
　*Shall see the antient us'd communion*
　*Of vowels, and consonants—*
FACE. 　　　　　　My master will heare!　20
DOL. *A wisedome, which* PYTHAGORAS *held most high—*
MAMMON. Sweet honorable lady.
DOL. 　　　　　　　　*To comprise*
　*All sounds of voyces, in few markes of letters—*
FACE. Nay, you must never hope to lay her now.

*They speake together.*

DOL. And so we may arrive
  by *Talmud* skill,
And profane *greeke*, to
  raise the building up

Of HELENS house, against
  the *Ismaelite*,
King of *Thogarma*, and his
  *Habergions*

Brimstony, blew, and fiery;
  and the force

Of King ABADDON, and the
  Beast of *Cittim*:
Which *Rabbi* DAVID KIMCHI,
  ONKELOS,

And ABEN-EZRA doe
  interpret *Rome*.

FACE. How did you put her
  into't?
MAMMON. Alas I talk'd          25
  Of a fift *Monarchy* I would
  erect,
With the *Philosophers stone*
  (by chance) and shee
Fals on the other foure,
  straight.
FACE. Out of BROUGHTON!
  I told you so. 'Slid stop her
  mouth.
MAMMON. Is't best?
FACE. She'll never leave else.
  If the old man heare her,      30
  We are but *fæces*, ashes.
SUBTLE. ⟨*Within.*⟩ What's to
  doe there?
FACE. O, we are lost. Now she
  heares him, she is quiet.

*Enter* SUBTLE.

MAMMON. Where shall I hide me?

*Upon* SUBTLES *entry they disperse.*

SUBTLE.                    How! What sight is here!
Close deeds of darknesse, and that shunne the light!
Bring him againe. Who is he? What, my sonne!          35
O, I have liv'd too long.
MAMMON.                    Nay good, deare father,
There was no'unchast purpose.
SUBTLE.                    Not? and flee me,
When I come in?
MAMMON.            That was my error.
SUBTLE.                        Error?
Guilt, guilt, my sonne. Give it the right name. No marvaile,
If I found check in our *great worke* within,          40
When such affaires as these were managing!
MAMMON. Why, have you so?

SUBTLE.                    It has stood still this halfe houre:
  And all the rest of our *lesse workes* gone back.
  Where is the instrument of wickednesse,
  My lewd false drudge?
MAMMON.                    Nay, good sir, blame not him.          45
  Beleeve me, 'twas against his will, or knowledge.
  I saw her by chance.
SUBTLE.                    Will you commit more sinne,
  T'excuse a varlet?
MAMMON.                    By my hope, 'tis true, sir.
SUBTLE.  Nay, then I wonder lesse, if you, for whom
  The blessing was prepar'd, would so tempt heaven:          50
  And loose your fortunes.
MAMMON.                    Why, sir?
SUBTLE.                              This'll retard
  The *worke*, a month at least.
MAMMON.                    Why, if it doe,
  What remedie? but thinke it not, good father:
  Our purposes were honest.
SUBTLE.                    As they were,
  So the reward will prove.
                        *A great crack and noise within.*
                    How now! Aye me.          55
  God, and all Saints be good to us. What's that?

*Enter* FACE.

FACE.  O sir, we are defeated! all the *workes*
  Are flowne *in fumo*: every glasse is burst.
  Fornace, and all rent downe! as if a bolt
  Of thunder had beene driven through the house.          60
  *Retorts, Receivers, Pellicanes, Bolt-heads,*
  All strooke in shivers!
               SUBTLE *falls downe as in a swoune.*
             Helpe, good sir! Alas,
  Coldnesse, and death invades him. Nay, sir MAMMON,
  Doe the faire offices of a man! You stand,
  As you were readier to depart, then he.          65
                     *One knocks.*
  Who's there? My lord her brother is come.

MAMMON.                                                    Ha, *Lungs?*
FACE.   His coach is at the dore. Avoid his sight,
  For hee's as furious, as his sister is mad.
MAMMON.   Alas!
FACE.              My braine is quite un-done with the fume, sir,
  I ne'er must hope to be mine owne man againe.                    70
MAMMON.   Is all lost, *Lungs?* Will nothing be preserv'd,
  Of all our cost?
FACE.                   Faith, very little, sir.
  A peck of coales, or so, which is cold comfort, sir.
MAMMON.   O my voluptuous mind! I am justly punish'd.
FACE.   And so am I, sir.
MAMMON.                     Cast from all my hopes—          75
FACE.   Nay, certainties, sir.
MAMMON.                     By mine owne base affections.

                    S U B T L E  *seemes come to himselfe.*

SUBTLE.   O, the curst fruits of vice, and lust!
MAMMON.                                          Good father,
  It was my sinne. Forgive it.
SUBTLE.                        Hangs my roofe
  Over us still, and will not fall, ô justice,
  Upon us, for this wicked man!
FACE.                          Nay, looke, sir,          80
  You grieve him, now, with staying in his sight:
  Good sir, the nobleman will come too, and take you,
  And that may breed a *tragœdie.*
MAMMON.                          I'll goe.
FACE.   I, and repent at home, sir. It may be,
  For some good penance, you may ha'it, yet,          85
  A hundred pound to the boxe at *Bet'lem*—
MAMMON.                                    Yes.
FACE.   For the restoring such as ha'their wits.
MAMMON.                                    I'll do't.
FACE.   Ile send one to you to receive it.
MAMMON.                          Doe.
  Is no *projection* left?
FACE.                    All flowne, or stinks, sir.

                    IV. V. 82. nobleman] H.S.; noble man F; Noble man Q.

MAMMON.  Will nought be sav'd, that's good for med'cine, thinkst
    thou?                                        90
FACE.  I cannot tell, sir.  There will be, perhaps,
    Something, about the scraping of the shardes,
    Will cure the itch: ⟨*aside*⟩ though not your itch of mind, sir.
    It shall be sav'd for you, and sent home. Good sir,
    This way: for feare the lord should meet you.

                                          *Exit* MAMMON.
                                      FACE.    95
SUBTLE.
FACE.  I.
SUBTLE.  Is he gone?
FACE.                   Yes, and as heavily
    As all the gold he hop'd for, were in his bloud.
    Let us be light, though.
SUBTLE.               I, as balls, and bound
    And hit our heads against the roofe for joy:
    There's so much of our care now cast away.        100
FACE.  Now to our *Don*.
SUBTLE.         Yes, your yong widdow, by this time
    Is made a *Countesse*, FACE: Sh'has beene in travaile
    Of a yong heire for you.
FACE.              Good, sir.
SUBTLE.                Off with your case,
    And greet her kindly, as a bride-groome should,
    After these common hazards.
FACE.                Very well, sir.    105
    Will you goe fetch *Don* DIEGO off, the while?
SUBTLE.  And fetch him over too, if you'll be pleas'd, sir:
    Would DOL were in her place, to pick his pockets now.
FACE.  Why, you can doe it as well, if you would set to't.
    I pray you prove your vertue.
SUBTLE.             For your sake, sir.    110
                                      *Exeunt.*

### SCENE VI

*Enter* SURLY *and* DAME PLIANT.

SURLY.  Lady, you see into what hands, you are falne;
    Mongst what a nest of villaines! and how neere

Your honor was t'have catch'd a certaine clap
(Through your credulitie) had I but beene
So punctually forward, as place, time,                           5
And other circumstance would ha'made a man:
For yo'are a handsome woman: would yo'were wise, too.
I am a gentleman, come here disguis'd,
Onely to find the knaveries of this *Citadell*,
And where I might have wrong'd your honor, and have not,     10
I claime some interest in your love. You are,
They say, a widdow, rich: and I am a batcheler,
Worth nought: Your fortunes may make me a man,
As mine ha'preserv'd you a woman. Thinke upon it,
And whether, I have deserv'd you, or no.
PLIANT.                                    I will, sir.        15
SURLY.   And for these houshold-rogues, let me alone,
   To treat with them.

*Enter* SUBTLE.

SUBTLE.                    How doth my noble DIEGO?
   And my deare madame, *Countesse*? Hath the *Count*
   Beene courteous, lady? liberall? and open?
   *Donzell*, me thinkes you looke melancholike,             20
   After your *coitum*, and scurvy! True-ly,
   I doe not like the dulnesse of your eye:
   It hath a heavy cast, 'tis *upsee Dutch*,
   And say's you are a lumpish whore-master.
   Be lighter, I will make your pockets so.                  25

                         *He falls to picking of them.*

SURLY.   Will you, *Don* bawd, and pick-purse? How now? Reele
   you?
   Stand up sir, you shall find since I am so heavy,
   I'll gi'you equall weight.
SUBTLE.                    Helpe, murder!
SURLY.                                        No, sir.
   There's no such thing intended. A good cart,
   And a cleane whip shall ease you of that feare.           30
   I am the *Spanish Don*, that should be cossened,
   Doe you see? cossened? Where's your Captayne FACE?
   That parcell-broker, and whole-bawd, all raskall.

*Enter* FACE, ⟨*in his captain's costume.*⟩

FACE. HOW, SURLY!
SURLY.                    O, make your approach, good Captaine.
    I'have found, from whence your copper rings, and spoones          35
    Come, now, wherewith you cheate abroad in tavernes.
    'Twas here, you learn'd t'anoint your boot with brimstone,
    Then rub mens gold on't, for a kind of touch,
    And say 'twas naught, when you had chang'd the colour,
    That you might ha't for nothing? And this Doctor,                 40
    Your sooty, smoakie-bearded compeere, he
    Will close you so much gold, in a bolts-head,
    And, on a turne, convay (i'the stead) another
    With *sublim'd Mercurie*, that shall burst i'the heate,
    And flye out all *in fumo*? Then weepes MAMMON:                   45
    Then swounes his worship.
                                                    *Exit* FACE.

                        Or, he is the FAUSTUS,
    That casteth figures, and can conjure, cures
    Plague, piles, and poxe, by the *Ephemerides*,
    And holds intelligence with all the bawdes,
    And midwives of three shires? while you send in—                  50
    Captaine, (what is he gone?) dam'sells with child,
    Wives, that are barren, or, the waiting maide
    With the greene-sicknesse? Nay, sir, you must tarrie
    Though he be scap't; and answere, by the eares, sir.


                        SCENE VII

                *Enter* FACE *and* KASTRIL.

FACE. Why, now's the time, if ever you will quarrell
    Well (as they say) and be a true-borne child.
    The Doctor, and your sister both are abus'd.
KASTRIL. Where is he? which is he? he is a slave
    What ere he is, and the sonne of a whore. Are you                  5
    The man, sir, I would know?
SURLY.                        I should be loth, sir,
    To confesse so much.

KASTRIL.                    Then you lie, i'your throate.
SURLY.                                                    How?
FACE.  A very errant rogue, sir, and a cheater,
    Employd here, by another conjurer,
    That dos not love the Doctor, and would crosse him          10
    If he knew how—
SURLY.                    Sir, you are abus'd.
KASTRIL.                                        You lie:
    And 'tis no matter.
FACE.                    Well said, sir. He is
    The impudent'st raskall—
SURLY.                        You are indeed. ⟨*To* KASTRIL.⟩
                                Will you heare me, sir?
FACE.  By no meanes: Bid him be gone.
KASTRIL.                            Be gone, sir, quickly.
SURLY.  This's strange! ⟨*To* PLIANT.⟩ Lady, doe you informe
    your brother.                                            15
FACE.  There is not such a foyst, in all the towne,
    The Doctor had him, presently: and findes, yet,
    The *Spanish Count* will come, here. Beare up, SUBTLE.
SUBTLE.  Yes, sir, he must appeare, within this houre.
FACE.  And yet this rogue, would come, in a disguise,         20
    By the temptation of another spirit,
    To trouble our art, though he could not hurt it.
KASTRIL.                                        I,
    I know—⟨*To* PLIANT.⟩ Away, you talke like a foolish mauther.

                                    *Exit* PLIANT.

SURLY.  Sir, all is truth, she saies.
FACE.                        Doe not beleeve him, sir:
    He is the lying'st Swabber! Come your wayes, sir.          25
SURLY.  You are valiant, out of companie.
KASTRIL.                            Yes, how then, sir?

*Enter* DRUGGER, ⟨*with a piece of damask.*⟩

FACE.  Nay, here's an honest fellow too, that knowes him,
    And all his tricks. (Make good what I say, ABEL,
    This cheater would ha'cossen'd thee o'the widdow.)

He owes this honest DRUGGER, here, seven pound,                    30
He has had on him, in two-penny'orths of *tabacco*.

DRUGGER.    Yes sir. And h'has damn'd himselfe, three termes, to
    pay mee.

FACE.    And what do's he owe for *lotium*?

DRUGGER.                              Thirtie shillings, sir:
    And for sixe *syringes*.

SURLY.                    HYDRA of villanie!

FACE.    Nay, sir, you must quarrell him out o'the house.

KASTRIL.                                        I will.    35
    Sir, if you get not out o'dores, you lie:
    And you are a pimpe.

SURLY.                    Why, this is madnesse, sir,
    Not valure in you: I must laugh at this.

KASTRIL.    It is my humour: you are a Pimpe, and a Trig,
    And an AMADIS *de Gaule*, or a *Don* QUIXOTE.                    40

DRUGGER.    Or a Knight o'the *curious cox-combe*. Doe you see?

*Enter* ANANIAS.

ANANIAS.    Peace to the houshold.

KASTRIL.                              Ile keepe peace, for no man.

ANANIAS.    Casting of dollers is concluded lawfull.

KASTRIL.    ⟨*To* FACE.⟩ Is he the Constable?

SUBTLE.                    Peace, ANANIAS.

FACE.                                        No, sir.

KASTRIL.    Then you are an *Otter*, and a *Shad*, a *Whit*,    45
    A very *Tim*.

SURLY.                    You'll heare me, sir?

KASTRIL.                              I will not.

ANANIAS.    What is the motive?

SUBTLE.                    Zeale, in the yong gentleman,
    Against his *Spanish* slops—

ANANIAS.                    They are profane,
    Leud, superstitious, and idolatrous breeches.

SURLY.    New raskals!

KASTRIL.                    Will you be gone, sir?

ANANIAS.                                        Avoid *Sathan*,    50
    Thou art not of the light. That ruffe of pride,
    About thy neck, betrayes thee: 'and is the same

With that, which the uncleane birds, in *seventy-seven*,
Were seene to pranke it with, on divers coasts.
Thou look'st like *Antichrist*, in that leud hat.                    55
SURLY.  I must give way.
KASTRIL.                    Be gone, sir.
SURLY.                            But Ile take
A course with you—
ANANIAS.                (Depart, proud *Spanish* fiend)
SURLY.  Captain, and Doctor—
ANANIAS.                Child of perdition.
KASTRIL.                            Hence, sir.

                            *Exit* SURLY.

Did I not quarrell bravely?
FACE.                Yes, indeed, sir.
KASTRIL.  Nay, and I give my mind to't, I shall do't.          60
FACE.  O, you must follow, sir, and threaten him tame.
Hee'll turne againe else.
KASTRIL.                I'll re-turne him, then.

                            *Exit* KASTRIL.

FACE.  DRUGGER, this rogue prevented us, for thee:
We'had determin'd, that thou shouldst ha'come,
In a *Spanish* sute, and ha'carried her so; and he          65
A brokerly slave, goes, puts it on himselfe.
Hast brought the damaske?
DRUGGER.                Yes sir.
FACE.                            Thou must borrow,
A *Spanish* suite. Hast thou no credit with the players?
DRUGGER.  Yes, sir, did you never see me play the foole?
FACE.  I know not, NAB: ⟨*aside*⟩ thou shalt, if I can helpe it.    70
HIERONYMO's old cloake, ruffe, and hat will serve,
Ile tell thee more, when thou bringst'hem.

                            *Exit* DRUGGER.

SUBTLE *hath whisperd with him* ⟨*i.e.* ANANIAS⟩ *this while.*

ANANIAS.                        Sir, I know
The *Spaniard* hates the *Brethren*, and hath spies
Upon their actions: and that this was one
I make no scruple. But the holy *Synode*                    75

Have beene in prayer, and meditation, for it.
And 'tis reveal'd no lesse, to them, then me,
That casting of money is most lawfull.

SUBTLE.                                                     True.
But here, I cannot doe it; if the house
Should chance to be suspected, all would out,                    80
And we be lock'd up, in the tower, for ever,
To make gold there (for th'state) never come out:
And, then, are you defeated.

ANANIAS.                          I will tell
This to the *Elders*, and the weaker *Brethren*,
That the whole companie of the *Separation*                      85
May joyne in humble prayer againe.

SUBTLE.                                    (And fasting.)
ANANIAS. Yea, for some fitter place. The peace of mind
Rest with these walls.

SUBTLE.                   Thanks, courteous ANANIAS.

*Exit* ANANIAS.


FACE. What did he come for?
SUBTLE.                        About casting dollers,
Presently, out of hand. And so, I told him,                      90
A *Spanish* minister came here to spie,
Against the faithfull—

FACE.                        I conceive. Come SUBTLE,
Thou art so downe upon the least disaster!
How wouldst tho'ha'done, if I had not helpt thee out?

SUBTLE. I thanke thee FACE, for the angrie Boy, i-faith.         95
FACE. Who would ha'lookt, it should ha'beene that raskall?
SURLY? He had dy'd his beard, and all. Well, sir,
Here's damaske come, to make you a suit.

SUBTLE.                                    Where's DRUGGER?
FACE. He is gone to borrow me a *Spanish* habite,
Ile be the *Count*, now.

SUBTLE.                        But where's the widdow?        100
FACE. Within, with my lords sister: Madame DOL
Is entertayning her.

SUBTLE.                   By your favour, FACE,
Now shee is honest, I will stand againe.

FACE.  You will not offer it?
SUBTLE.                     Why?
FACE.                                     Stand to your word,
   Or—here comes DOL. She knowes—
SUBTLE.                                     Yo'are tyrannous still.  105
FACE.  Strict for my right.

*Enter* DOL.

                     How now, DOL? Hast'told her,
   The *Spanish Count* will come?
DOL.                                     Yes, but another is come,
   You little look'd for!
FACE.                     Who's that?
DOL.                                     Your master:
   The master of the house.
SUBTLE.                     How, DOL!
FACE.                                     Shee lies.
   This is some trick. Come, leave your quiblins, DOROTHEE.  110
DOL.  Looke out, and see.
SUBTLE.                     Art thou in earnest?
DOL.                                     'Slight,
   Fortie o'the neighbours are about him, talking.
FACE.  ⟨*At window.*⟩ 'Tis he, by this good day.
DOL.                                     'Twill prove ill day,
   For some on us.
FACE.                     We are undone, and taken.
DOL.  Lost, I'am afraid.
SUBTLE.                     You said he would not come,  115
   While there dyed one a weeke, within the liberties.
FACE.  No: 'twas within the walls.
SUBTLE.                                     Was't so? Cry'you mercy:
   I thought the liberties. What shall we doe now, FACE?
FACE.  Be silent: not a word, if he call, or knock.
   I'll into mine old shape againe, and meet him,  120
   Of JEREMIE, the butler. I'the meane time,
   Doe you two pack up all the goods, and purchase,
   That we can carry i'the two trunkes. I'll keepe him
   Off for today, if I cannot longer: and then
   At night, Ile ship you both away to *Ratcliffe*,  125

Where wee'll meet to morrow, and there wee'll share.
Let MAMMON's brasse, and pewter keepe the cellar:
Wee'll have another time for that. But, DOL,
'Pray thee, goe heate a little water, quickly,
SUBTLE must shave me. All my Captaines beard                    130
Must off, to make me appeare smooth JEREMIE.
You'll do't?
SUBTLE.              Yes, Ile shave you, as well as I can.
FACE.  And not cut my throte, but trim me?
SUBTLE.                              You shall see, sir.

                                        *Exeunt.*


# ACT V

## SCENE I

*Enter* LOVE-WIT *and* NEIGHBOURS.

LOVE-WIT.  Has there beene such resort, say you?
FIRST NEIGHBOUR.                         Daily, sir.
SECOND NEIGHBOUR.  And nightly, too.
THIRD NEIGHBOUR.                  I, some as brave as lords.
FOURTH NEIGHBOUR.  Ladies, and gentlewomen.
FIFTH NEIGHBOUR.                   Citizens wives.
FIRST NEIGHBOUR.  And knights.
SIXTH NEIGHBOUR.            In coches.
SECOND NEIGHBOUR.            Yes, and oyster-women.
FIRST NEIGHBOUR.  Beside other gallants.
THIRD NEIGHBOUR.                   Sailors wives.
FOURTH NEIGHBOUR.                    *Tabacco*-men.    5
FIFTH NEIGHBOUR.  Another *Pimlico*!
LOVE-WIT.              What should my knave advance,
    To draw this companie? He hung out no banners
    Of a strange Calfe, with five legs, to be seene?
    Or a huge Lobster, with six clawes?
SIXTH NEIGHBOUR.              No, sir.
THIRD NEIGHBOUR.  We had gone in then, sir.

LOVE-WIT.                                    He has no guift   10
  Of teaching i'the nose, that ere I knew of!
  You saw no Bills set up, that promis'd cure
  Of agues, or the tooth-ach?
SECOND NEIGHBOUR.            No such thing, sir.
LOVE-WIT.   Nor heard a drum strooke, for Babiouns, or Puppets?
FIFTH NEIGHBOUR.   Neither, sir.
LOVE-WIT.                What device should he bring forth now!   15
  I love a teeming wit, as I love my nourishment.
  'Pray god he ha'not kept such open house,
  That he hath sold my hangings, and my bedding:
  I left him nothing else. If he have eate'hem,
  A plague o'the moath, say I. Sure he has got   20
  Some bawdy pictures, to call all this ging;
  The Frier, and the Nun; or the new *Motion*
  Of the Knights courser, covering the Parsons mare;
  The Boy of sixe yeere old, with the great thing:
  Or't may be, he has the Fleas that runne at tilt,   25
  Upon a table, or some Dog to daunce?
  When saw you him?
FIRST NEIGHBOUR.   Who sir, JEREMIE?
SECOND NEIGHBOUR.                JEREMIE butler?
  We saw him not this mon'th.
LOVE-WIT.                How!
FOURTH NEIGHBOUR.                Not these 5. weeks, sir.
THIRD NEIGHBOUR.   These six weeks, at the least.
LOVE-WIT.                    Yo'amaze me, neighbours!
FIFTH NEIGHBOUR.   Sure, if your worship know not where he is,   30
  Hee's slipt away.
SIXTH NEIGHBOUR.   Pray god, he be not made away!
LOVE-WIT.   Ha? It's no time to question, then.

                                    *He knocks.*

SIXTH NEIGHBOUR.                    About
  Some three weekes since, I heard a dolefull cry,
  As I sate up, a mending my wives stockings.
LOVE-WIT.   This's strange! that none will answere! Didst thou
  heare   35

v. I. 29 THIRD NEIGHBOUR] NEI. Q, F, YALE: NEI. 6. F2. H.S. *give the line to
the first neighbour, but the third has not spoken for some time.*

A cry, saist thou?

SIXTH NEIGHBOUR.  Yes, sir, like unto a man
     That had been strangled an houre, and could not speake.

SECOND NEIGHBOUR.  I heard it too, just this day three weekes,
          at two a clock
     Next morning.

LOVE-WIT.          These be miracles, or you make'hem so!       40
     A man an houre strangled, and could not speake,
     And both you heard him cry?

THIRD NEIGHBOUR.          Yes, downeward, sir.

LOVE-WIT.  Thou art a wise fellow: Give me thy hand, I pray
     thee.

     What trade art thou on?

THIRD NEIGHBOUR.          A smith, and't please your worship.

LOVE-WIT.  A smith? Then, lend me thy helpe, to get this dore
     open.

THIRD NEIGHBOUR.  That I will presently, sir, but fetch my
     tooles—                                                   45

                              *Exit* THIRD NEIGHBOUR.

FIRST NEIGHBOUR.  Sir, best to knock againe, afore you breake
     it.


### SCENE II

*Enter* FACE, *dressed as a butler.*

LOVE-WIT.  I will.

FACE.          What meane you, sir?

FIRST, SECOND, and
FOURTH NEIGHBOURS.          O, here's JEREMIE!

FACE.  Good sir, come from the dore.

LOVE-WIT.          Why! what's the matter?

FACE.  Yet farder, you are too neere, yet.

LOVE-WIT.          I' the name of wonder!
     What meanes the fellow?

FACE.          The house, sir, has beene visited.

LOVE-WIT.  What? with the plague? stand thou then farder.

FACE.                              No, sir,       5
     I had it not.

LOVE-WIT.        Who had it then? I left
   None else, but thee, i'the house!
FACE.                                Yes, sir. My fellow,
   The cat, that kept the buttry, had it on her
   A weeke, before I spied it: but I got her
   Convay'd away, i'the night. And so I shut    10
   The house up for a month—
LOVE-WIT.                        How!
FACE.                                Purposing then, sir,
   T'have burnt rose-vinegar, triackle, and tarre,
   And, ha'made it sweet, that you should ne'er ha' knowne it:
   Because I knew the newes would but afflict you, sir.
LOVE-WIT. Breath lesse, and farder off. Why, this is stranger!  15
   The neighbours tell me all, here, that the dores
   Have still been open—
FACE.                        How, sir!
LOVE-WIT.                                Gallants, men, and women,
   And of all sorts, tag-rag, beene seene to flock here
   In threaves, these ten weekes, as to a second *Hogs-den*,
   In dayes of *Pimlico*, and *Eye-bright*!
FACE.                                Sir,    20
   Their wisedomes will not say so!
LOVE-WIT.                                To day, they speake
   Of coaches, and gallants; one in a *French*-hood,
   Went in, they tell me: and another was seene
   In a velvet gowne, at the windore! diverse more
   Passe in and out!
FACE.                        They did passe through the dores then,  25
   Or walls, I assure their eye-sights, and their spectacles;
   For here, sir, are the keyes: and here have beene,
   In this my pocket, now, above twentie dayes!
   And for before, I kept the fort alone, there.
   But, that 'tis yet not deepe i'the after-noone,    30
   I should beleeve my neighbours had seene double
   Through the black-pot, and made these apparitions!
   For, on my faith, to your worship, for these three weekes,
   And upwards, the dore has not beene open'd.
LOVE-WIT.                                Strange!
FIRST NEIGHBOUR.  Good faith, I thinke I saw a coach!

SECOND NEIGHBOUR.                              And I too, 35
  I'lld ha'beene sworne!
LOVE-WIT.                  Doe you but thinke it now?
—And but one coach?
FOURTH NEIGHBOUR.  We cannot tell, sir: JEREMIE
  Is a very honest fellow.
FACE.                        Did you see me at all?
FIRST NEIGHBOUR.  No. That we are sure on.
SECOND NEIGHBOUR.                  I'll be sworne o'that.
LOVE-WIT.  Fine rogues, to have your testimonies built on!          40

*Enter* THIRD NEIGHBOUR.

THIRD NEIGHBOUR.  Is JEREMIE come?
FIRST NEIGHBOUR.              O, yes, you may leave your tooles,
  We were deceiv'd, he sayes.
SECOND NEIGHBOUR.              He'has had the keyes:
  And the dore has beene shut these three weekes.
THIRD NEIGHBOUR.                  Like enough.
LOVE-WIT.  Peace, and get hence, you changelings.
FACE.  ⟨*Looking off-stage*⟩                  SURLY come!
  And MAMMON made acquainted? They'll tell all.          45
  (How shall I beate them off? What shall I doe?)
  Nothing's more wretched, then a guiltie conscience.


### SCENE III

*Enter* SURLY *and* MAMMON.

SURLY.  No, sir, he was a great physitian. This,
  It was no bawdy-house: but a meere *Chancell.*
  You knew the lord, and his sister.
MAMMON.                  Nay, good SURLY—
SURLY.  The happy word, *be rich*—
MAMMON.                  Play not the tyranne—
SURLY.  Should be to day pronounc'd, to all your friends.          5
  And where be your andirons now? and your brasse pots?
  That should ha'beene golden flaggons, and great wedges?
MAMMON.  Let me but breath. What! They ha'shut their dores,
  Me thinks!

SURLY.   I, now, 'tis holy-day with them.

                          MAMMON *and* SURLY *knock.*
MAMMON.                          Rogues,
   Coseners, impostors, bawds.
FACE.                          What meane you, sir?                    10
MAMMON.   To enter if we can.
FACE.                          Another mans house?
   Here is the owner, sir. Turne you to him,
   And speake your businesse.
MAMMON.                          Are you, sir, the owner?
LOVE-WIT.   Yes, sir.
MAMMON.          And are those knaves, within, your cheaters?
LOVE-WIT.   What knaves? what cheaters?
MAMMON.                          SUBTLE, and his *Lungs.*   15
FACE.   The gentleman is distracted, sir! No lungs,
   Nor lights ha'beene seene here these three weekes, sir,
   Within these dores, upon my word!
SURLY.                          Your word,
   Groome arrogant?
FACE.                Yes, sir, I am the house-keeper,
   And know the keyes ha'not beene out o'my hands.          20
SURLY.   This's a new FACE?
FACE.                          You doe mistake the house, sir!
   What signe was't at?
SURLY.                You raskall! This is one
   O'the confederacie. Come, let's get officers,
   And force the dore.
LOVE-WIT.                'Pray you stay, gentlemen.
SURLY.   No, sir, wee'll come with warrant.
MAMMON.                          I, and then,          25
   We shall ha'your dores open.

                          *Exeunt* MAMMON *and* SURLY.

LOVE-WIT.                          What meanes this?
FACE.   I cannot tell, sir!
FIRST NEIGHBOUR.          These are two o'the gallants,
   That we doe thinke we saw.
FACE.                          Two o'the fooles?

You talke as idly as they. Good faith, sir,
I thinke the *Moone* has cras'd'hem all!

*Enter* KASTRIL.

(O me,                                                        30
The angrie Boy come too? Hee'll make a noyse,
And nere away till he have betray'd us all.)

KASTRIL *knocks.*

KASTRIL.  What rogues, bawds, slaves, you'll open the dore anone,
Punque, cocatrice, my suster. By this light
I'll fetch the marshall to you. You are a whore,         35
To keepe your castle—
FACE.                    Who would you speake with, sir?
KASTRIL.  The bawdy Doctor, and the cosening Captaine,
And Pus my suster.
LOVE-WIT.          This is something, sure!
FACE.  Upon my trust, the dores were never open, sir.
KASTRIL.  I have heard all their tricks, told me twice over,    40
By the fat knight, and the leane gentleman.

*Enter* ANANIAS *and* TRIBULATION.

LOVE-WIT.  Here comes another.
FACE.                    ANANIAS too?
And his *Pastor?*
TRIBULATION.  The dores are shut against us.

*They beat too, at the dore.*

ANANIAS.  Come forth, you seed of sulphure, sonnes of fire,
Your stench, it is broke forth: abomination            45
Is in the house.
KASTRIL.          I, my suster's there.
ANANIAS.                    The place,
It is become a cage of uncleane birds.
KASTRIL.  Yes, I will fetch the scavenger, and the constable.
TRIBULATION.  You shall doe well.
ANANIAS.                    Wee'll joyne, to weede them out.
KASTRIL.  You will not come then? punque, device, my suster!   50
ANANIAS.  Call her not sister. Shee is a harlot, verily.
KASTRIL.  I'll raise the street.

LOVE-WIT.                    Good gentlemen, a word.
ANANIAS.   *Sathan*, avoid, and hinder not our zeale.

*Exeunt* KASTRIL, ANANIAS *and* TRIBULATION.

LOVE-WIT.   The world's turn'd *Bet'lem*.
FACE.                              These are all broke loose,
  Out of S. KATHER'NES, where they use to keepe,          55
  The better sort of mad-folkes.
FIRST NEIGHBOUR.              All these persons
  We saw goe in, and out, here.
SECOND NEIGHBOUR.           Yes, indeed, sir.
THIRD NEIGHBOUR.   These were the parties.
FACE.                         Peace, you drunkards. Sir,
  I wonder at it! Please you, to give me leave
  To touch the dore, I'll trie, an'the lock be chang'd.          60

⟨FACE *goes to the door.*⟩

LOVE-WIT.   It mazes me!
FACE.              Good faith, sir, I beleeve,
  There's no such thing. 'Tis all *deceptio visus*.
  Would I could get him away.

DAPPER *cryes out within.*

DAPPER.              Master Captayne, master Doctor.
LOVE-WIT.   Who's that?
FACE.          (Our clark within, that I forgot!) I know not, sir.
DAPPER.   For gods sake, when wil her *Grace* be at leisure?
FACE.                                        Ha!   65
  Illusions, some spirit o'the aire: (his gag is melted,
  And now he sets out the throte.)
DAPPER.              I am almost stiffled—
FACE.   (Would you were altogether.)
LOVE-WIT.                  'Tis i'the house.
  Ha! List.
FACE.        Beleeve it, sir, i'the aire!
LOVE-WIT.                  Peace, you—
DAPPER.   Mine aunts *Grace* do's not use me well.
SUBTLE.   ⟨*Within.*⟩                  You foole,   70
  Peace, you'll marre all.
FACE.              Or you will else, you rogue.

LOVE-WIT. O, is it so? Then you converse with spirits!
  Come sir. No more o'your tricks, good JEREMIE,
  The truth, the shortest way.
FACE.               Dismisse this rabble, sir.
  What shall I doe? I am catch'd.
LOVE-WIT.             Good neighbours,    75
  I thanke you all. You may depart.

                   *Exeunt* NEIGHBOURS.

                 Come sir,
  You know that I am an indulgent master:
  And therefore, conceale nothing. What's your med'cine,
  To draw so many severall sorts of wild-fowle?
FACE. Sir, you were wont to affect mirth, and wit:    80
  (But here's no place to talke on't i'the street.)
  Give me but leave, to make the best of my fortune,
  And onely pardon me th'abuse of your house:
  It's all I begge. I'll helpe you to a widdow,
  In recompence, that you shall gi'me thankes for,    85
  Will make you seven yeeres yonger, and a rich one.
  'Tis but your putting on a *Spanish* cloake,
  I have her within. You need not feare the house,
  It was not visited.
LOVE-WIT.      But by me, who came
  Sooner then you expected.
FACE.             It is true, sir.    90
  'Pray you forgive me.
LOVE-WIT.        Well: let's see your widdow.

                       *Exeunt.*


SCENE IV

*Enter* SUBTLE, *and* DAPPER *blindfolded.*

SUBTLE.  How! ha' you eaten your gag?
DAPPER.               Yes faith, it crumbled
  Away i'my mouth.
SUBTLE.        You ha'spoil'd all then.
DAPPER.                No,
  I hope my aunt of *Faery* will forgive me.
    E

SUBTLE.   Your aunt's a gracious lady: but in troth
 You were to blame.
DAPPER.                    The fume did over-come me,                    5
 And I did do't to stay my stomack. 'Pray you
 So satisfie her *Grace*.

*Enter* FACE.

SUBTLE.                    Here comes the Captaine.
FACE.   How now! Is his mouth downe?
SUBTLE.                                        I! he has spoken!
FACE.   (A poxe, I heard him, and you too.) Hee's un-done, then.
 (I have beene faine to say, the house is haunted                    10
 With spirits, to keepe churle back.
SUBTLE.                                        And hast thou done it?
FACE.   Sure, for this night.
SUBTLE.                    Why, then triumph, and sing
 Of FACE so famous, the precious king
 Of present wits.
FACE.                    Did you not heare the coyle,
 About the dore?
SUBTLE.                    Yes, and I dwindled with it.)                    15
FACE.   Shew him his aunt, and let him be dispatch'd:
 I'll send her to you.

           *Exit* FACE.

SUBTLE.                    Well sir, your aunt her *Grace*,
 Will give you audience presently, on my sute,
 And the Captaines word, that you did not eate your gag,
 In any contempt of her *Highnesse*.

        ⟨*Unbinds his eyes.*⟩
DAPPER.                    Not I, in troth, sir.                    20

*Enter* DOL *like the Queene of Faery.*

SUBTLE.   Here shee is come. Downe o'your knees, and wriggle:
 Shee has a stately presence. Good. Yet neerer,
 And bid, God save you.
DAPPER.                    Madame.
SUBTLE.                                        And your aunt.

---

v. iv. 7. SUBTLE] Q, F *and editors give the line to Dapper, but he is still blind-folded, since he cannot be allowed to see Face as Jeremy, and therefore cannot recognise him.*

DAPPER.  And my most gracious aunt, god save your *Grace*.

DOL.  Nephew, we thought to have beene angrie with you:                25
 But that sweet face of yours, hath turn'd the tide,
 And made it flow with joy, that eb'd of love.
 Arise, and touch our velvet gowne.

SUBTLE.                              The skirts,
 And kisse'hem. So.

DOL.                      Let me now stroke that head,
 *Much, nephew, shalt thou win; much shalt thou spend;*                30
 *Much shalt thou give away: much shalt thou lend.*

SUBTLE.  (I, much, indeed.) Why doe you not thanke her *Grace*?

DAPPER.  I cannot speake, for joy.

SUBTLE.                              See, the kind wretch!
 Your *Graces* kins-man right.

DOL.                      Give me the *Bird*.
 Here is your *Fly* in a purse, about your neck, cosen,                35
 Weare it, and feed it, about this day sev'night,
 On your right wrist—

SUBTLE.                      Open a veine, with a pinne,
 And let it suck but once a weeke: till then,
 You must not looke on't.

DOL.                      No. And, kins-man,
 Beare your selfe worthy of the bloud you come on.                40

SUBTLE.  Her grace would ha'you eate no more *Wool-sack* pies,
 Nor *Dagger* frume'ty.

DOL.                      Nor breake his fast,
 In *heaven*, and *hell*.

SUBTLE.                      Shee's with you every where!
 Nor play with Costar-mongers, at *mum-chance*, *tray-trip*,
 *God make you rich*, (when as your aunt has done it:) but keepe                45
 The gallant'st company, and the best games—

DAPPER.                              Yes, sir.

SUBTLE.  *Gleeke* and *primero*: and what you get, be true to us.

DAPPER.  By this hand, I will.

SUBTLE.                      You may bring's a thousand pound,
 Before to morrow night, (if but three thousand
 Be stirring) an'you will.

DAPPER.                      I sweare, I will then.                50

   49. thousand<sub>∧</sub>] ~, F, H.S.; Thousand<sub>∧</sub> Q.

SUBTLE.  Your *Fly* will learne you all games.

FACE.  ⟨*Within.*⟩                              Ha'you done there?

SUBTLE.  Your grace will command him no more duties?

DOL.                                                       No:

But come, and see me often. I may chance
To leave him three or foure hundred chests of treasure,
And some twelve thousand acres of *Faerie* land:                    55
If he game well, and comely, with good gamesters.

SUBTLE.  There's a kind aunt! kisse her departing part.
But you must sell your fortie marke a yeare, now.

DAPPER.  I, sir, I meane.

SUBTLE.                        Or, gi't away: pox on't.

DAPPER.  I'le gi't mine aunt. Ile goe and fetch the writings.          60

SUBTLE.  'Tis well, away.

                                                *Exit* DAPPER.

*Enter* FACE.

FACE.                          Where's SUBTLE?

SUBTLE.                                    Here. What newes?

FACE.  DRUGGER is at the doore, goe take his suite,
And bid him fetch a Parson, presently:
Say, he shall marrie the widdow. Thou shalt spend
A hundred pound by the service!

                                                *Exit* SUBTLE.
                          Now, queene DOL,                    65

Ha'you pack'd up all?

DOL.                    Yes.

FACE.                          And how doe you like
The lady PLYANT?

DOL.                    A good dull innocent.

*Enter* SUBTLE, ⟨*with Spanish costume.*⟩

SUBTLE.  Here's your HIERONIMO's cloake, and hat.

FACE.                                        Give mee'hem.

SUBTLE.  And the ruffe too?

FACE.                          Yes, I'll come to you presently.

                                                *Exit* FACE.

SUBTLE.  Now, he is gone about his project, DOL,                    70
I told you of, for the widow.

                    58. your] Q; you F.

DOL.                          'Tis direct
  Against our articles.
SUBTLE.                    Well, wee'll fit him, wench.
  Hast thou gull'd her of her jewels, or her bracelets?
DOL.  No, but I will do't.
SUBTLE.                    Soone at night, my DOLLY,
  When we are shipt, and all our goods aboord,                    75
  East-ward for *Ratcliffe*; we will turne our course
  To *Brainford*, westward, if thou saist the word:
  And take our leaves of this ore-weaning raskall,
  This peremtorie FACE.
DOL.                    Content, I'am weary of him.
SUBTLE.  Tho'hast cause, when the slave will runne a wiving, DOL,  80
  Against the instrument, that was drawne betweene us.
DOL.  I'll plucke his bird as bare as I can.
SUBTLE.                          Yes, tell her,
  She must by any meanes, addresse some present
  To th'cunning man; make him amends, for wronging
  His art with her suspition; send a ring;                    85
  Or chaine of pearle; shee will be tortur'd else
  Extremely in her sleepe, say: and ha'strange things
  Come to her. Wilt thou?
DOL.                    Yes.
SUBTLE.                    My fine flitter-mouse,
  My bird o'the night; wee'll tickle it at the *pigeons*,
  When we have all, and may un-lock the trunkes,                    90
  And say, this's mine, and thine, and thine, and mine—
                             *They kisse.*

*Enter* FACE.

FACE.  What now, a billing?
SUBTLE.                    Yes, a little exalted
  In the good passage of our stock-affaires.
FACE.  DRUGGER has brought his Parson, take him in, SUBTLE,
  And send NAB back againe, to wash his face.                    95
SUBTLE.  I will: and shave himselfe?
FACE.                    If you can get him.
                            *Exit* SUBTLE.

DOL.  You are hot upon it, FACE, what ere it is!

FACE.  A trick, that DOL shall spend ten pound a month by.

*Enter* SUBTLE.

   Is he gone?

SUBTLE.          The Chaplaine waits you i'the hall, sir.

FACE.  I'll goe bestow him.

                                 *Exit* FACE.

DOL.          Hee'll now marry her, instantly.          100

SUBTLE.  He cannot, yet, he is not readie. Deare DOL,
   Cosen her of all thou canst. To deceive him
   Is no deceipt, but justice, that would breake
   Such an inextricable tye as ours was.

DOL.  Let me alone to fit him.

*Enter* FACE.

FACE.          Come, my venturers,          105
   You ha'pack'd up all? Where be the trunkes? Bring forth.

SUBTLE.  Here.

FACE.          Let's see'hem. Where's the money?

SUBTLE.          Here,·
   In this.

FACE.          MAMMONS ten pound: eight score before.
   The *Brethrens* money, this. DRUGGERS, and DAPPERS.
   What paper's that?

DOL.          The jewell of the waiting maides,          110
   That stole it from her lady, to know certaine—

FACE.  If shee should have precedence of her mistris?

DOL.          Yes.

FACE.  What boxe is that?

SUBTLE.          The fish-wives rings, I thinke:
   And th'ale-wives single money. Is't not DOL?

DOL.  Yes: and the whistle, that the saylors wife          115
   Brought you, to know, and her husband were with WARD.

FACE.  Wee'll wet it to morrow: and our silver-beakers,
   And taverne cups. Where be the *French* petti-coats,
   And girdles, and hangers?

SUBTLE.          Here, i'the trunke,
   And the bolts of lawne.

FACE.          Is DRUGGERS damaske, there?          120
   And the *tabacco*?

SUBTLE.            Yes.
FACE.                        Give me the keyes.
DOL.  Why you the keyes!
SUBTLE.                        No matter, DOL: because
    We shall not open'hem, before he comes.
FACE.  'Tis true, you shall not open them, indeed:
    Nor have'hem forth. Doe you see? Not forth, DOL.
DOL.                                              No!    125
FACE.  No, my smock-rampant. The right is, my master
    Knowes all, has pardon'd me, and he will keepe'hem.
    Doctor, 'tis true (you looke) for all your figures:
    I sent for him, indeed. Wherefore, good partners,
    Both hee, and shee, be satisfied: for, here                130
    Determines the *indenture tripartite*,
    Twixt SUBTLE, DOL, and FACE. All I can doe
    Is to helpe you over the wall, o'the back-side;
    Or lend you a sheet, to save your velvet gowne, DOL.
    Here will be officers, presently; bethinke you,          135
    Of some course sodainely to scape the dock:
    For thether you'll come else.

                                        *Some knock.*

                    Harke you, thunder.
SUBTLE.  You are a precious fiend!
OFFICER.  ⟨*Within.*⟩                Open the dore.
FACE.  DOL, I am sorry for thee i-faith. But hearst thou?
    It shall goe hard, but I will place thee some-where:      140
    Thou shalt ha'my letter to mistris AMO.
DOL.                                  Hang you—
FACE.  Or madame *Cæsarean*.
DOL.                        Poxe upon you, rogue,
    Would I had but time to beat thee.
FACE.                              SUBTLE,
    Let's know where you set up next; I'll send you
    A customer, now and then, for old acquaintance:          145
    What new course ha'you?
SUBTLE.                      Rogue, I'll hang my selfe:
    That I may walke a greater divell, then thou,
    And haunt thee i'the flock-bed, and the buttery.

                                        *Exeunt.*

## SCENE V

*Enter* LOVE-WIT *in Spanish costume.*

OFFICERS, MAMMON, SURLY, KASTRIL, ANANIAS,
*and* TRIBULATION *are heard shouting within.*

LOVE-WIT.   What doe you meane, my masters?
MAMMON.                              Open your dore,
  Cheaters, bawds, conjurers.
OFFICER.                    Or wee'll breake it open.
LOVE-WIT.   What warrant have you?
OFFICER.                    Warrant inough, sir, doubt not:
  If you'll not open it.
LOVE-WIT.              Is there an officer, there?
OFFICER.   Yes, two, or three for fayling.
LOVE-WIT.                    Have but patience,          5
  And I will open it straight.

*Enter* FACE.

FACE.        Sir, ha'you done?
  Is it a marriage? perfect?
LOVE-WIT.              Yes, my braine.
FACE.   Off with your ruffe, and cloake then, be your selfe, sir.

                    ⟨LOVE-WIT *removes his disguise.*⟩

SURLY.   Downe with the dore.
KASTRIL.                    'Slight, ding it open.
LOVE-WIT.                              Hold.
  Hold gentlemen, what meanes this violence?          10

                    ⟨*He opens the door; the rest rush in.*⟩

MAMMON.   Where is this Colliar?
SURLY.                    And my Captaine FACE?
MAMMON.   These day-Owles.
SURLY.                    That are birding in men purses.
MAMMON.   Madame *Suppository.*
KASTRIL.                    *Doxey*, my suster.

ANANIAS.　　　　　　　　　　　　　　　　Locusts
　　Of the foule pit.
TRIBULATION.　　　Profane as BEL., and the *Dragon*.
ANANIAS.　Worse then the Grasse-hoppers, or the Lice of *Egypt*.　　15
LOVE-WIT.　Good gentlemen, heare me. Are you officers,
　　And cannot stay this violence?
OFFICER.　　　　　　　　　　Keepe the peace.
LOVE-WIT.　Gentlemen, what is the matter? Whom doe you seeke?
MAMMON.　The *Chymicall* cousoner.
SURLY.　　　　　　　　　　And the Captaine *Pandar*.
KASTRIL.　The *Nun* my suster.
MAMMON.　　　　　　　　　　Madame *Rabbi*.
ANANIAS.　　　　　　　　　　　　　Scorpions,　　20
　　And Caterpillers.
LOVE-WIT.　　　　　Fewer at once, I pray you.
OFFICER.　One after another, gentlemen, I charge you,
　　By vertue of my staffe—
ANANIAS.　　　　　　　　They are the vessells
　　Of pride, lust, and the cart.
LOVE-WIT.　　　　　　　　Good zeale, lie still,
　　A little while.
TRIBULATION.　Peace, Deacon ANANIAS.　　　　　　25
LOVE-WIT.　The house is mine here, and the dores are open:
　　If there be any such persons, as you seeke for,
　　Use your authoritie, search on o'gods name.
　　I am but newly come to towne, and finding
　　This tumult 'bout my dore (to tell you true)　　　　30
　　It somewhat maz'd me; till my man, here, (fearing
　　My more displeasure) told me he had done
　　Somewhat an insolent part, let out my house
　　(Belike, presuming on my knowne aversion
　　From any aire o'the towne, while there was sicknesse)　　35
　　To a Doctor, and a Captaine: who, what they are,
　　Or where they be, he knowes not.
MAMMON.　　　　　　　　Are they gone?

32. he had] F2; had Q, F.

LOVE-WIT.   You may goe in, and search, sir.

*They enter ⟨the interior of the house; KASTRIL and*
                                    *SURLY remain.⟩*

                        Here, I find

The emptie walls, worse then I left'hem, smok'd,
A few crack'd pots, and glasses, and a fornace,                    40
The seeling fill'd with *poesies* of the candle:
And MADAME, with a *Dildo*, writ o'the walls.
Onely, one gentlewoman, I met here,
That is within, that said shee was a widdow—

KASTRIL.   I, that's my suster. I'll goe thumpe her. Where is shee?   45

                                    *Exit* KASTRIL.

LOVE-WIT.   And should ha'marryed a *Spanish Count*, but he,
When he came to't, neglected her so grosly,
That I, a widdower, am gone through with her.

SURLY.   How! Have I lost her then?

LOVE-WIT.                                  Were you the *Don*, sir?
Good faith, now, shee do's blame yo'extremely, and sayes   50
You swore, and told her, you had tane the paines,
To dye your beard, and umbre o'er your face,
Borrowed a sute, and ruffe, all for her love;
And then did nothing. What an over-sight,
And want of putting forward, sir, was this!                    55
Well fare an old Hargubuzier, yet,
Could prime his poulder, and give fire, and hit,
All in a twinckling.

MAMMON *comes forth.*

MAMMON.                   The whole nest are fled!

LOVE-WIT.   What sort of birds were they?

MAMMON.                                  A kind of Choughes,
Or theevish Dawes, sir, that have pickt my purse              60
Of eight-score, and ten pounds, within these five weekes,
Beside my first materialls; and my goods,
That lye i'the cellar: which I am glad they ha'left,
I may have home yet.

LOVE-WIT.                   Thinke you so, sir?

MAMMON.                                  I.

63. left,] Q, H.S.; ~. F.

LOVE-WIT.  By order of law, sir, but not otherwise.                    65

MAMMON.  Not mine owne stuffe?

LOVE-WIT.                              Sir, I can take no knowledge,
    That they are yours, but by publique meanes.
    If you can bring certificate, that you were gull'd of'hem,
    Or any formall writ, out of a court,
    That you did cosen your selfe: I will not hold them.                    70

MAMMON.  I'll rather loose'hem.

LOVE-WIT.                              That you shall not, sir,
    By me, in troth. Upon these termes they'are yours.
    What should they ha'beene, sir, turn'd into gold all?

MAMMON.                                                    No.
    I cannot tell. It may be they should. What then?

LOVE-WIT.  What a great losse in hope have you sustain'd?                    75

MAMMON.  Not I, the common-wealth has.

FACE.                              I, he would ha'built
    The citie new; and made a ditch about it
    Of silver, should have runne with creame from *Hogsden*:
    That, every sunday in *More*-fields, the younkers,
    And tits, and tom-boyes should have fed on, *gratis*.                    80

MAMMON.  I will goe mount a turnep-cart, and preach
    The end o'the world, within these two months. SURLY,
    What! in a dreame?

SURLY.                              Must I needs cheat my selfe,
    With that same foolish vice of honestie!
    Come let us goe, and harken out the rogues.                    85
    That FACE I'll marke for mine, if ere I meet him.

FACE.  If I can heare of him, sir, I'll bring you word,
    Unto your lodging: for in troth, they were strangers
    To me, I thought'hem honest, as my selfe, sir.

*Exeunt* MAMMON *and* SURLY.

*They* ⟨*i.e.* ANANIAS *and* TRIBULATION⟩ *come forth.*

TRIBULATION.  'Tis well, the *Saints* shall not loose all yet. Goe,                    90
    And get some carts—

LOVE-WIT.                              For what, my zealous friends?

ANANIAS.  To beare away the portion of the righteous,
    Out of this den of theeves.

LOVE-WIT.                What is that portion?

ANANIAS.   The goods, sometimes the Orphanes, that the *Brethren*
Bought with their silver pence.

LOVE-WIT.                    What, those i'the cellar,          95
The knight sir MAMMON claimes?

ANANIAS.                        I doe defie
The wicked MAMMON, so doe all the *Brethren*,
Thou prophane man. I aske thee, with what conscience
Thou canst advance that Idol, against us,
That have the seale? Were not the shillings numbred,          100
That made the pounds? Were not the pounds told out,
Upon the second day of the fourth weeke,
In the eight month, upon the table dormant,
The yeere, of the last patience of the *Saints*,
Sixe hundred and ten?

LOVE-WIT.              Mine earnest vehement botcher,          105
And *Deacon* also, I cannot dispute with you,
But, if you get you not away the sooner,
I shall confute you with a cudgell.

ANANIAS.                      Sir.

TRIBULATION.   Be patient ANANIAS.

ANANIAS.                      I am strong,
And will stand up, well girt, against an host,          110
That threaten GAD in exile.

LOVE-WIT.              I shall send you
To *Amsterdam*, to your cellar.

ANANIAS.                      I will pray there,
Against thy house: may dogs defile thy walls,
And waspes, and hornets breed beneath thy roofe,
This seat of false-hood, and this cave of cos'nage.          115

*Exeunt* ANANIAS *and* TRIBULATION.

DRUGGER *enters* ⟨*with the* PARSON⟩, *and he beats him away.*

LOVE-WIT.   Another too?

DRUGGER.                Not I sir, I am no *Brother*.

LOVE-WIT.   Away you HARRY NICHOLAS, doe you talke?

*Exit* DRUGGER.

FACE.  No, this was ABEL DRUGGER.

To the Parson.

Good sir, goe,

And satisfie him; tell him, all is done:
He stay'd too long a washing of his face.　　　　　120
The Doctor, he shall heare of him at *Westchester*;
And of the Captayne, tell him at *Yarmouth*: or
Some good port-towne else, lying for a winde.

Exit PARSON.

If you get off the angrie Child, now, sir—

*Enter* KASTRIL, ⟨*speaking*⟩ *to his sister.*

KASTRIL.  Come on, you yew, you have match'd most sweetly,
　　ha'you not?　　　　　125
　　Did not I say, I would never ha'you tupt
　　But by a dub'd Boy, to make you a lady-*Tom*?
　　'Slight, you are a mammet! O, I could touse you, now.
　　Death, mun'you marry with a poxe?

LOVE-WIT.　　　　　　　　　You lie, Boy;
　　As sound as you: and I am afore-hand with you.

KASTRIL.　　　　　　　　Anone?　　130

LOVE-WIT.  Come, will you quarrell? I will feize you, sirrah.
　　Why doe you not buckle to your tooles?

KASTRIL.　　　　　　　Gods light!
　　This is a fine old Boy, as ere I saw!

LOVE-WIT.  What, doe you change your copy, now? Proceed,
　　Here stands my dove: stoupe at her, if you dare.　　135

KASTRIL.  'Slight I must love him! I cannot choose, i-faith!
　　And I should be hang'd for't. Suster, I protest,
　　I honor thee, for this match.

LOVE-WIT.　　　　　　O, doe you so, sir?

KASTRIL.  Yes, and thou canst take *tabacco*, and drinke, old Boy,
　　I'll give her five hundred pound more, to her marriage,　　140
　　Then her owne state.

LOVE-WIT.　　　　　Fill a pipe-full, JEREMIE.

FACE.  Yes, but goe in, and take it, sir.

LOVE-WIT.　　　　　　　We will.
　　I will be rul'd by thee in any thing, JEREMIE.

KASTRIL.  'Slight, thou art not hide-bound! thou art a *Jovy*'Boy!
  Come let's in, I pray thee, and take our whiffes.                         145
LOVE-WIT.  Whiffe in with your sister, brother Boy.

>                         *Exeunt* KASTRIL *and* PLIANT.
>                                   That master
  That had receiv'd such happinesse by a servant,
  In such a widdow, and with so much wealth,
  Were very ungratefull, if he would not be
  A little indulgent to that servants wit,                                  150
  And helpe his fortune, though with some small straine
  Of his owne candor. Therefore, gentlemen,
  And kind Spectators, if I have out-stript
  An old mans gravitie, or strict canon, thinke
  What a yong wife, and a good braine may doe:                              155
  Stretch ages truth sometimes, and crack it too.
  Speake for thy selfe, knave.
FACE.                         So I will, sir. Gentlemen,
  My part a little fell in this last *Scene*,
  Yet 'twas *decorum*. And though I am cleane
  Got off, from SUBTLE, SURLY, MAMMON, DOL,                                 160
  Hot ANANIAS, DAPPER, DRUGGER, all
  With whom I traded; yet I put my selfe
  On you, that are my countrey: and this pelfe,
  Which I have got, if you doe quit me, rests
  To feast you often, and invite new ghests.

---

# THE END.

---

This Comoedie was first
acted, in the yeere
1610.
*By the Kings Majesties*
SERVANTS.

The principall Comœdians were,

| | |
|---|---|
| RIC. BURBADGE. | JOH. HEMINGS. |
| JOH. LOWIN. | WILL. OSTLER. |
| HEN. CONDEL. | JOH. UNDERWOOD. |
| ALEX. COOKE. | NIC. TOOLY. |
| ROB. ARMIN. | WILL. EGLESTONE. |

*With the allowance of the Master of* REVELLS.

# TEXTUAL NOTES

The following notes are selective only. They include readings from texts other than F only where these have substantive value, or throw light on the processes of correction and revision.

## SIGLA

Q = Quarto, 1612.
Qᵘ = Quarto, 1612 (uncorrected).
Qᶜ = Quarto, 1612 (corrected).
F = Folio, 1616.
Fᵘ = Folio, 1616 (uncorrected).
Fᶜ = Folio, 1616 (corrected).
F2 = Folio, 1640.
F3 = Folio, 1692.
YALE = *The Alchemist*, ed. C. M. Hathaway. New York (Yale U.P.) 1903.
H.S. = *Ben Jonson*, ed. C. H. Herford, Percy and Evelyn Simpson. Oxford (Oxford U.P.) 1925–52.
*om.* = omits, is omitted by.
~ = form of word(s) cited in lemma.

### DEDICATION

DESERVING . . . BLOUD:] F; æquall with vertue, / *and her Blood*: / The Grace, and Glory of women. Q.

4-5 *how might . . . they have*] F; how, yet, might a gratefull minde be furnish'd against the iniquitie of *Fortune*; except, when she fail'd it, it had power to impart it selfe? A way found out, to ouercome euen those, whom *Fortune* hath enabled to returne most, since they, yet leaue themselues more. In this assurance am I planted; and stand with those affections at this Altar, as shall no more auoide the light and witnesse, then they doe Q.

6 *vertue?*] F; vertue. Q.

7 *value . . . which*] F; valew, that Q.

9    *as . . . are*] F; in these times Q.
10   *assiduitie*] F; daylinesse Q.
11   *This, yet*] F; But this Q.


EPISTLE

*Text from* Q; *om.* F.
4    Age)] Q^c; ~, Q^u.
5–6  *Daunces, and Antickes*] Q^c;
     *Iigges, and Daunces* Q^u.
14   *Many*] Q^c; *Multitude* Q^u.


DRAMATIS PERSONAE

Play] F; Comœdie Q.
SURLY, DOL, KASTRIL] F
*gives these forms in the text of
the play, but here gives* SURLEY,
DOL., KASTRILL. (Q *gives*
SURLY, DOL:, KASTRIL.)
DAME] DA. F; Da: Q.
THE SCENE/LONDON.] F;
*om.* Q.


PROLOGUE

10   for] F; to Q.


I. I

11   slave.] F; ~, Q, H.S.
25   corner.] F; ~, H.S.; Corner, Q.
55   and] Q, F; *and* H.S.
69   call'd our] F; the *high* Q^c; Q^u *as*
     Q^c, *but does not italicise* "*third
     region*" *or* "*high . . . grace*".
92   (O . . . all.)] F; Q *om. brackets.*
108  ruin'd! lost!] F; ~_∧ ~. Q.
114  barbing it.] F; *barbing.* Q.
134  equalitie] F; æqualitie Q. *Similar
     spelling variations recur else-
     where, and are not further noted.*
148  Death on me! ]F; Gods will! Q.


I. II

4    I, I'am] F; I am Q.
15   you.] Q^c, F; ~_∧ Q^u; ~, F3.

45   meate] F; mouth Q.
56   XENOPHON] F; *Testament* Q—
     *a blasphemy change.*
135  JOVE] F; Gad Q.
137  fac's] F; fac is Q.
140  Slight] Q, F; *but* F *spacing suggests
     that* J. *wrote* 'Slight.


I. III

32   gold-smith] F; Goldmith Q.
44   *metaposcopie* F, YALE; *Metapos-
     copie* Q; *metoposcopie* H.S.
59   *Ormus*] F; *Ormu's* Q.
67   *Mercurial*] F; *Mercurian* Q.
85   'nd] F; And Q; and F2; '⟨a⟩nd
     H.S.


I. IV

16   possess'd] F; possess'd on't Q.


II. I

4    *Ophir*] Q^c, F; *Ophyr* Q^u.
4    to't,] F; ~_∧ Q.
25   FACE. (*Within*) Sir.] {*Within*}
     Sir. F; {*WITHIN*} Sir. Q; *in
     both* Q, F *set to right of text,
     between* ll. 25 *and* 24, *without
     speech-heading.*
27   lungs] F; Lungs Q.
76   water?] Q^c, F; ~, Q^u.


II. II

12   stuffe, inough_∧] Q, F; H.S. *con-
     jecture* stuffe_∧ inough, (*noting*
     F2 stuffe_∧ enough_∧).
13   Buy] F; Take Q.
24   bleard-eyes] F; bleard eyes Q.
40   *and*] F; & Q; and F2, H.S.
58–9 They . . . others.] F; *om.* Q.
60   pure] F; best Q.
62   poets,] H.S.; ~_∧ F; Poets_∧ Q, F2.

## II. III

32   Ulen spiegel] F; *Vlen spiegle* Q.

36   Which,] H.S.; ~‿ Q, F.

70–1   (O . . . pitching.)] F2; F
      *places first bracket before speech-
      heading;* Q *om. brackets. So also
      at ll.* 80–1., *except* F2 *as* F.

83   H.] F2, H.S.; ~‿ F; H. Q.

88   I . . . bolted?] Q, F; H.S. *bracket
      as at ll.* 70–1, 80–1.

176   mettalls] F; Mettall Q.

210   DOL *is seene.*] F; *also in* Q.

218   returnes] F; *some copies show as*
      "return s".

221–2   Stay man . . . hether—] *Order
      of lines as* Q, H.S.; *lines trans-
      posed in* F, F2, YALE. *Davis (see
      above p.* 10) *defends* F, *but* Q
      *gives better sense. In l.* 221 Q
      *has the speech-heading* FAC. *for*
      MAM.

225   god] F; God Q. *This distinction
      is general throughout, and is not
      further noted.*

238   BRAUGHTONS] F; *Broughtons*
      Q.

249   Come‿] Q; ~, F, H.S.

249   Ulen] F; Zephyrus Q.

260   Ulen] F (*without speech-heading*);
      *om.* Q.

271   trecherou'st] F^c; treacherou'st
      F^u (H.S., IX, p. 70), Q.

272   her,] F, F2; ~‿ Q. F *indicates an
      ironical pause, cf.* IV. III. 75.

282   And‿] F3, H.S. (=An; *cf.* II. V.
      60); ~, Q, F, F2.

313   you?] F; ~. Q.

315   Ulen] F; *om.* Q.

## II. IV

6   WHA'TS'HUMS] F; *Whachums*
     Q; WHATS'HUM'S H.S.

7   statelich] F; statelich Q.

11   Sanguine] Q^c, F; sanguine Q^u.

## II. V

10   stiptick] H.S., YALE; *stipstick* Q, F;
      *styptick* F2.

29   Malleation.] Q, F^c; ~, F^u (H.S.,
      IX, p. 70).

53   SUBTLE.] SVB. F; SVR. Q.

55   penn'orth.] Q, F; ~, F2, H.S.,
      YALE.

60   And‿] H.S.; ~, Q, F (cf. II. III.
      282).

## II. VI

8–9   ('Slight . . . more.)] F; Q *om.
      brackets.*

24   FACE.] FAC. F; *om.* Q.

38   (his . . . too!)] F; Q *om. brackets.*

40   NAB, *send*] H.S.; NAB, Send F;
      *Nab!* Send Q.

74   Stay] Q^c, F; Say Q^u.

92   ha'] Q, F (*most copies*); ~‿ F
      (*ed.'s copy*).

## III. I

2–4   And . . . frailties] F; And such
      rebukes th'*Elect* must beare,
      with patience; / They are the
      exercises of the Spirit, / And
      sent to tempt our fraylties. Q.

15   are,] Q, H.S.; ~‿ F.

## III. II

35   paintings] F; painting Q.

36   Talck;] H.S.; Talck:Q; Talek; F.

72   bonds] F; Bandes Q.

99   glorious] F; *holy* Q.

107   them—] F; 'hem. Q.

120   There‿] ~, Q, F, H.S.; *probably
      connected with l.* 122.

122   They'are] Q, H.S.; ~‿ ~ F.

135   you'll] F; you shall Q.

## III. III

1   caustive] F; costive Q.

17   (That . . . colour,)] F; Q *om.
      brackets.*

22 milke] F; feele Q.
42 sees] H.S.; see's Q, F.
62 FACE.] FAC. F2; *om.* Q, F.
72 DOLLY.] H.S.; ~∧ F; *Dolly.* Q.
79 Lett's] F; Lett's vs Q.
80 *cues*] F; QQˢ Q.

### III. IV

2 (I . . . it)] F; Q *om. brackets.*
4 (he sayes.)] F; *om.* Q.
8 DRUGGER.] NAB. F; *Nab.* Q
   (DRV. *normally in both*).
60 *baronie*] F; *Baronry* Q.
75 'Od's] F; God's Q.
76–8 (can . . . afore-hand)] F; Q
   *om. brackets.*
84 long)] *Read by one copy of* F
   *recorded by* H.S. (IX, p. 71) *and
   also the New York copy. In both
   this page is otherwise uncorrected.
   Other copies, in which this page
   is otherwise corrected, read "long
   (". Probably connected with error
   of bracket at l. 92. (Q reads
   "long)", but with italic brackets.)*
92 That] Q; (That F.
92 without∧] Fᶜ, Q; ~, Fᵘ (H.S.
   IX, p. 71).
132 goe.] F; goe, Sir. Q.
133–4 (SUBTLE . . . her.)] F; Q *om.
   brackets.*

### III. V

24–8 (If . . . un-done.)] F; Q *om.
   brackets.*
68 (shee sayes)] F; , she sayes, Q.

### IV. I

6 o'] F; on Q.
18 Ullen] F; *Lungs* Q.
38, 39 (Well . . . bird.), (O . . .
   idolatrie!)] F; Q *om. brackets.*
95 nature.] ~: F, H.S.; *Nature:* Q.
101 *solæcisme*] Q, F; *solœcisme* H.S.

107 the light] F; light Q.
112 in] F; of Q.
145 POPPÆA] F2; POPPÆA F;
   *Poppæa* Q.
155 with all] Q, F; withall F2, *perhaps
   correctly.*
171 laboratory] H.S.; *Laboratory* Q;
   labaratory F.

### IV. II

1 cleare.] Q, Fᶜ; ~∧ Fᵘ (H.S., IX,
   p. 71).
7 cortine] F, F2; Curtine Q; Cur-
   tain F3.
28 this!] F; ~∧ Q, H.S.

### IV. III

11 'Slight] F; 'Sblood Q.
21 beso las] Q, F2; besolas F.
31 *Madrid*] F; *Madril* Q.
81–2 call, . . . hinges.] Q, H.S.; ~.
   ~, F.
89 to∧ you] F; ~' ~ Q, H.S.

### IV. IV

3 FACE.] FAC. Q; *om.* F.
17–19 (For . . . shortly.)] F; Q *om.
   brackets.*
77 *A llegar*] H.S.; *Alle gar* Q, F.
80 *entremus*] Q, F; *entremos* H.S.

### IV. V

1–23 For . . . letters] *Italics as* F;
   Q *italicises only proper names and
   a few other words.*
25–32 And so . . . quiet.] Q, F *print
   in small type in two columns,
   separated by braces. Cropped
   copies of Q lack some words.* F2
   *prints in one column; italic in
   large paper copies* (H.S.).
25, 29 MAMMON.] MAM. Q, F2;
   MAN. F.

27   With] F; Which Q.
30   ABADDON] F2, H.S.; ABADDON
     F; *Abaddon* Q.
31   DAVID] F2, H.S.; DAVID F;
     *Dauid* Q.
31   *fæces*] F2; *fœces* Q, F.
42–3  stood still . . . gone back] F;
     gone back . . . stand still Q.
51   This'll retard] F; This will
     hinder Q.


             IV. VI

16   SURLY.] SVR. Q; SVB. F.


             IV. VII

28–9  (Make . . . ABEL, . . .
     widdow.)] H.S.; (Make . . .
     ABEL,) . . . widdow. F; Make . . .
     *Abel,* . . . Widdow. Q.
32   h'has] F; he hath Q.
47   motive?] H.S.; motiue! F; Motiue.
     Q.
57   fiend)] Fᶜ; ~. Fᵘ (H.S., IX, p. 71
     *and New York copy*); *Fiend.* Q,
     *which om. brackets.* F *also places
     first bracket before speech-heading,
     likewise at l. 86 and* V. III. 68; *cf.*
     II. III. 70–1.
65   he‸] Q, F; ~, H.S.
81   tower] F; Tower Q.
104  SUBTLE.] SVB. Q; SVR. F.
126  there] F; then Q.


              V. I

28   mon'th] H.S.; mont'h Q, F;
     month YALE.
42   hand,] Q, F (*ed.'s copy, very
     faint*); ~‸ F (*most copies*).


              V. II

36   I'lld] Q, F; I'll F2; I'ld H.S.
42   keyes:] Qᶜ, F; ~, Qᵘ.


              V. III

32 S.D.   KASTRIL] *Kastrill* F.
33   anone,] F; ~. Q, H.S.
44–5  seed . . . is] F; Seed of Vipers,
     Sonnes of *Belial,* / Your wicked-
     nesse is Q.
46   I, my] F; My Q.
48   Yes] F; I Q.
81   (But . . . street.)] F; Q *om.*
     *brackets.*


              V. IV

4    troth] F; truth Q.
10–5  (I . . . it.)] F; Q *om. brackets.*
23   you] F; her Q.
32   (I . . . indeed.)] F; Q *om.*
     *brackets.*
42   frume'ty] F; Frumenty Q.
44   *trip,*] Q, H.S.; ~. F.
50   an'] F; if Q.
55   twelve] F; fiue Q.
58   now.] Q; ~: F, H.S.
59   pox] F; A poxe Q.
60   DAPPER.] DAP. F2; FAC. Q, F.
95   NAB] F; him Q.
127  'hem.] Q; ~, F.
138  SUBTLE.] SVB. Q; SYB. F.
142  *Cæsarean*] F; *Imperiall* Q.


              V. V

24   pride . . . cart] F shame, and of
     dishonour Q.
63   ha'] F; haue Q.
94   *Brethren‸*] Q, H.S.; ~, F.
99   Idol] F; *Nemrod* Q.
105  ten?] F2; ~. F; tenne. Q.
118  *To the Parson.*] F *refers this to
     the speech-heading* FAC. *by an
     asterisk.*
144  *Jovy'*] F; *Iouy* Q.
145  I pray] F; pray Q.


        LIST OF ACTORS

This . . . REVELLS.] F; *om.* Q.

# COMMENTARY

## DEDICATION

LA. WROTH] Niece of Sir P. Sidney, patroness of letters, to whom J. addressed *Epigrams* ciii, cv, *Underwoods* xxviii; l. 8 suggests she was concerned in the conception of the play.

l. 13 *Faces*] J. sees Face as a "hollow man".

## EPISTLE

Much of this reappears in *Discoveries* (H.S., X, p. 51); the source is largely Quintilian, and the critical opinions typical of J.

l. 5 *Concupiscence . . . Antickes*] The phrase, in its Qᵘ form ("Iigges, and Daunces") reappears in the Induction to *Bartholomew Fair* (ll. 127–32) in a similar passage usually thought to be an attack on *The Tempest* and *Winter's Tale*. If the Epistle also refers to Shakespeare, was it omitted from F because of his recent death?

## DRAMATIS PERSONAE

l. 15 Mutes] As Officers and Neighbours are specified, only the Parson of v. IV is identifiable. Perhaps the "good wives" of I. III are seen on stage; but cf. Introduction, p. 7.

## PROLOGUE

l. 9 manners] Not "social behaviour or eccentricity", but "conduct in its moral aspect", demonstrating the moral basis of the humours theory. Cf. *The Magnetic Lady*, Induction, ll. 99–111, and see J. D. Redwine (Bibliography).

## I. I

6 wild sheepe] The dangerous stuff in the phial; the alchemist can be called "pastor", and his substance his "sheep".

16 livery . . . thrum] A servant whose uniform is made of loose ends of cloth (thrum) and earns only £3 a year.

18 vacations] The law-court terms (l. 139) were the busy periods of London life.

19 suburb-Captayne] Bawd or pandar, brothels being located in the suburbs outside the control of the city.

25 *pie-corner*] An eating area in Smithfield, so called from an inn sign.

29 *romane* wash] A lotion; "romane" perhaps = pale, or grimy.

31 *artillerie-yard*] The Tower gunners trained at this yard (or "garden") near Bishopsgate.

52 buttry-hatch etc.] Doles of beer and scraps were distributed to the poor from the rich man's buttery.

54 vailes] Gamesters were expected to tip the butler, especially at Christmas, and to buy counters from him for card games such as "post and pair".

62 tempest] The explosive mixture

in the phial; by alchemical metaphor, =thunder and lightning.

69   *third region*] The higher, purer region, as of the upper levels of the air.

74   dimensions] Cf. II. VI. 65 ff., IV. II. 16 ff.; =measurements, rules for "scientific" control of duelling.

83   *equi clibanum*] Low temperature furnace, warmed by horse-dung, =*fimus equinus*, III. II. 139.

90   colliar] Colliers were black, and therefore of the devil, and renowned for giving false weights, cf. V. V. 11.

94   hollow cole] See Chaucer, *Canon's Yeoman's Tale*, for details of the trick.

95   sive, and sheeres] A sort of "dowsing" device for discovering lost articles and thieves.

97   shaddowes . . . glasse] Reflections in a crystal or beryl, consulted in divination.

98   red letters] Used for emphasis in old printing.

99   RATSEY] A highwayman, executed 1605, publicised by using a hideous mask.

106   lying . . . basket] Eating more than a fair share of scraps provided for prisoners.

112   *statute*] Act of 1541 (also 1403) forbidding alchemical making of gold and silver.

114   laundring . . . barbing] Washing gold in acid and clipping it.

129   feather] Blackfriars was a puritan district, and the centre of the feather trade.

152   *Sol*, and *Luna*] The two main alchemical principles, gold and silver, male and female, king and queen, corresponding to the two "planets", the sun and moon.

168   hole . . . eare-rent] Stand in the pillory without ears.

170   *Don Provost*] The executioner.

175   CLARIDIANA] Heroine of the popular romance *The Mirror of Knight-hood*.

191   dagger] Inn and gaming-house, cf. V. IV. 42.

### I. II

17   *Reade*] Dr Simon Read of Southwark, pardoned in 1608 for employing spirits to recover stolen money.

26   *Chiause*] Turkish *chaush* = "herald". One Mustafa, calling himself a *chaush*, swindled London merchants in 1607, and was received at court; hence "chouse" = "to cheat".

46   CLIM . . . CLOUGHS] Heroic outlaw of northern ballad origin. CLARIBEL] A false knight in Spenser, *Fairy Queen*, IV. IX.

47   *five . . . flush*] The best hands at primero.

61   velvet head] Pun on a doctor's velvet cap, and the "velvet" of a deer's horns.

79   *puppit*-play] See *Bartholomew Fair*, V. IV. for an example

99   mouth . . . score] His friends will all eat on credit at the eating-houses.

109   HOLLAND] John and John Isaac Holland, father and son, Dutch 15th century alchemists. As their works were not published till 1600, J. may have thought that Isaac was still living.

112   cloke] Strip them to their cloaks.

### I. III

4   Free] A member of the Grocers' Company.

28   lilly pots . . . juniper] Drugger has all the fashionable fittings: flowered jars, a block for shredding tobacco, tongs for hot coals, and

the best brands of fire-wood and pipes.

36   clothing . . . scarlet . . . fine] He will wear the Company's livery, be made sheriff, and pay the fine for refusing the office.

53   thumbe . . . ballance] Alchemy, palmistry and astrology are allied by the use of the planetary system. H.S. observe that Subtle's diagnosis is here falsified, to bring in Mercury, god of commerce.

65   *Mathlai . . . Thiel*] Spirit names from the *Elementa Magica Pietri de Abano*, 1567 (?) (H.S.).

72   puppet . . . vice] Doll worked by machinery.

## I. IV

14   *magisterium*] Master-work: the "great work" changes metals to gold, the "less" to silver; cf. II. V. 36.

21   pomander-bracelets] A traditional protection against plague, consisting of aromatic substances.

## II. I

4   *Ophir*] Solomon traditionally sailed to Ophir to make gold there alchemically—a tale denounced as foolish by del Rio (ed. of 1657, p. 70).

9   hollow . . . card] Loaded dice and crooked cards.

12   Seale] The "commodity" swindle, by which a borrower takes part of his loan in (worthless) goods; here, the whore is used to persuade him to sign. Cf. Epistle, and III. IV. 90.

17   AUGUSTA] Presumably a brothel-keeper.

26   fire-drake . . . lungs] "Lungs" =an alchemist's drudge; later, Mammon uses it as a nick-name.

"Fire-drake" (=fiery serpent, meteor, or fire-work) is a humorous equivalent.

33   *Lothbury*] A street of copper-founders and braziers.

41   *infinitum*] The stone has the power of "multiplication" (cf. mustard-seed, l. 60), of rejuvenation (l. 53) and universal healing (l. 64); and the biblical patriarchs, as shown by their longevity, knew its secret.

56   fifth age] *i.e.* of the seven traditionally allotted to Man.

62   *Pickt-hatch*] A prostitutes' area near the Charterhouse; cf. *Every Man in his Humour* I. II.

76   water-worke] Stow records the piping of Thames water to private houses in 1582 and 1594.

81   MOSES] Mammon's bibliography is orthodox: *e.g.* Moses' sister, Maria Prophetissa, wrote a *Practica*, and Solomon a *Liber de Lapide*, and J. himself owned a ms. of Solomon's *Opus de Arte Magica*, now B.M. Sloane 313. Some held High Dutch to be the language spoken in Eden.

89   fleece . . . thigh . . . tub] From del Rio, who disapproved of the view that they were alchemical treatises—"libros . . . in membranis arietinis descriptos" (ed. 1657, p. 71, cf. l. 91).

93   MEDEAS charmes] Especially, her broth for rejuvenating Aeson.

95 ff.   *argent-vive* etc.] Most of these parallels are in Robertus Vallensis (H.S., X, p. 72). *Argentum vivum fixum* and *Draco* are given as synonyms for the stone by Gratarolus (*Verae Alchemiae Doctrina*, 1561, p. 265). The alchemical story of Danae is used by Lyly in *Gallathea*, II. III. For Demogorgon =chaos=*quinta essentia*=*argentum vivum*=the source of all

things, see E. H. Duncan (bibliography).

## II. II

9  wench] Not merely a joke, but a
reference to the alchemical metaphor of procreation and birth.

23  beech] Cf. Chaucer, *Canon's
Yeoman's Tale*, l. 375; alchemical
fire had to be of beech-wood, for
a steady heat.

25  colours] Various colours indicate
the stages attained. The green
lion can be equated with gold,
the peacock's tail (Argus) means
a combination of colours, black and
white are stages on the way to the
final red, and birds can represent
substances or stages. The red *sanguis agni* implies the identification
with the body of Christ.

43  TIBERIUS] He had rooms decor-
ated with amatory drawings from
the writer Elephantis, otherwise
unknown. Aretino wrote *Sonnetti
Lussuriosi* for a like set of drawings
by Giulio Romano. There is a
Roman background for most of
Mammon's sensual visions.

63  *fart*] A famous 17th-century
anthology piece of 1607 which
records an embarrassing incident
in the Commons, printed in
*Musarum Deliciae*, 1656.

77  APICIUS] A Roman glutton, to
whom was ascribed a (later) col-
lection of recipes, in ten books.

97  *frugi*] "Austere"; it was a common-
place that the stone could be won
only by a pious man, "nec cupidus,
nec avarus" (Geber).

## II. III

10  hast] Haste was a cardinal error
in alchemy, repeatedly denounced.

29  *robe*] Substances may be des-
cribed as "clothed" when they put
on a particular colour; cf. shirt, l.83.

30  *triple Soule*] The stone, being
perfect, unites in itself the *tria
prima*, spirit, soul and body =
sulphur, mercury, salt (? = Subtle,
Face, Dol); cf. II. v. 41.

32  Ulen ſpiegel] Tyll Owlglass, jest-
book hero of a German tale
published in England *c.* 1528;
alchemy was associated with Ger-
many especially through Faustus
and Paracelsus.

44  *wheele*] The cyclic nature of the
alchemical process is often sym-
bolised by a wheel.

46  *Sulphur o'nature*] Sulphur in its
theoretically perfect red state.

50  colledges etc.] Nicholas Flamel,
mediaeval French alchemist, did
in fact provide such charities.

97  inferiour workes] Metaphorically,
Dapper and Drugger are in
fixation, Mammon in ascension.

101  sallad] An acceptable metaphor
for alchemical compounds; so
"vinegar" (l. 100) = *lac virginis*.

106 ff.  iterate] This account of "iter-
ation" or "multiplication" is from
Arnaldus' *Rosarium Philosophorum*:
cf. II. I. 38.

131-176  egge . . . mettalls] This
central debate is a transcription,
often verbatim, from del Rio,
*Disquisitiones Magicae* I, lxxxiii.

164  *hermaphrodeitie*] The figure of a
hermaphrodite is used to symbolise
the conjoined substances by *e.g.*
Mylius, *Philosophia Reformata*,
1622.

180  game] Alchemy is called a *lusus*,
or *lusus puerorum*, and *ludi Mer-
curiales* = amalgamation of silver
and mercury. Cards too appear in
alchemical interiors, probably as
symbols; this may be why Surly
is a "gamester".

184–207 *elixir . . . allegories*] Again from del Rio, with some help from Geber. *Chrysosperme* is seed of gold, *marchesite* pyrites, *tutie* impure zinc, *magnesia* sometimes mercury and tin, *toad* base matter, *panther* a spotted colour, *firmament* the "planetary" relationships, or the space within a circular vessel, *adrop* lead, *lato* a dark mixed metal, *azoch* mercury, *zernich* orpiment, *chibrit* sulphur, *heautarit* mercury, *termes* menstrual flow (literal or symbolic). Symbols, parables and allegories are standard excuses for obscurity.

225 BRADAMANTE] An Amazonian heroine from Ariosto's *Orlando Furioso*.

230–3 *Paracelsian . . . * GALEN] Traditional medicine was based on the herbal doctrines of Galen (2nd century A.D.). The great pre-chemist Theophrastus of Hohenheim, or Paracelsus (1493–1541), opened the door to using mineral substances in medicine, and was regarded as a sinister magician.

238 BRAUGHTON] Hugh Broughton (1549–1612), puritanical divine, Hebraist and chronologer; see on IV. V. 1 ff., where he is parodied.

287 *quick-silver . . . sulphur*] Medicines for venereal and skin diseases.

320 *Bantam*] City of Java, newly opened up, and suggestive of oriental wealth.

329 chaine . . . vermine] Chain worn by a great Lord's steward—sign of promotion to the top rank of "vermine", punning on "ermine".

## II. IV

20 *Anabaptist*] This sect, originally German (1521), abjured infant baptism, and advocated community of goods and a theocracy.

30 *Amsterdam*] Puritans driven from England took refuge in the Low Countries.

## II. V

8 *Lullianist . . . Ripley*] Raymond Lull or Lully (1235–1315), Spanish alchemist and inventor; Canon Sir George Ripley of Bridlington, died c. 1490, author of *Compound of Alchemy* and *Medulla Alchemiae*, in limping verse.

10 *sapor*] Taste, like colour, was a guide to progress made; "pontic" is sour, and "styptic" astringent.

13 KNIPPER-DOLING] Bernt Knipperdollinck, a leader of the Anabaptist rising in Münster (1534).

20 vexations . . . martyrizations] Substances are said to be tortured (cf. *supplicium*, *l.* 29) and "martyred"; hence they can be thought of as "heroes", and perhaps identified with "saints", like Ananias' brethren.

28 *trine . . . spheares*] Paracelsus states that a substance in solution must circulate three times within the "firmament" of the seven alchemical spheres.

29 passion . . . *Malleation*] Geber describes the specific "passion" (quality of endurance) of metals as that of spreading by hammering— "sub malleo . . . extensibile". (*Summa Perfectionis*, xxxi).

30 *Antimonium*] A very loose term, perhaps used here because antimony renders gold less malleable.

31 *Mercury*] Called *servus fugitivus*, "runaway slave" or "servant": Face is metaphorically a type of mercury.

## II. VI

2   *Baiards*] Charlemagne's blind horse which proverbially thrust boldly in anywhere; cf. *Canon's Yeoman's Tale*, l. 860.

20   DEE] Dr John Dee (1527–1608), astrologer, mathematician, and alchemist, employed by Queen Elizabeth.

33   hood] Court ladies wore hats; but this hood was worn high on head ("a cop"), not flat—perhaps a half-way stage towards the mode.

## III. I

8   marke of the *Beast*] Subtle's velvet cap; and *Revelations* XIX, 20.

21   Cookes] The cook is also a symbol of the alchemist.

38   *silenc'd Saints*] In 1604, at the Hampton Court conference, clergymen who denied various points of Anglican orthodoxy were forbidden to hold services.

## III. II

31   incombustible] Oil that does not burn was one of the alchemists' triumphs.

45   massie] Subtle defiantly repeats the offending syllable.

69–82   vizard . . . *Starch*] Standard charges against Puritans; hawking and starch, for instance, are abhorred by Stubbes.

138   *ignis ardens* etc.] Very hot fire, by contrast with the milder *fimus equinus* (see comment on I. I. 83), *balnei* (bath) and *cineris* (ash) heats.

146   third examination] Gold was tested three times, "probata satis triplum" (Geber).

150   no Magistrate] Many Puritans rejected all secular authority in "religious" matters, a doctrine open to wide abuse.

## III. III

2   round] The circular (l. 64) concourse of the Temple Church, see II. III. 289.

24   JOHN LEYDENS] John Bockelson of Leyden was a leader of the Münster Anabaptist rising of 1534; cf. II. V. 13.

33   say . . . campe] Dol quotes the opening line of *The Spanish Tragedy*, linking with later references to Hieronymo (IV. VII).

41   *Dousabell*] Dulcibella (=sweetheart), a name probably taken from pastoral poetry; but "Dowzabell" is one of the "upright men", or sturdy knaves, named by Harman in *Caveat for Common Cursitors* (1566), (A. V. Judges, *Elizabethan Underworld*, p. 110).

46   frost] 1607–8, when the Thames was frozen over.

49   *Gods-guift*] The etymological (Greek) sense of "Dorothea".

64   circle] The "round" of the Temple church, punning on the necromancer's magic circle.

## III. IV

25   *Duello* etc.] Satirising the contemporary punctilio of "scientific" duelling, set out *e.g.* in *Vincentio Saviolo his Practise*, 1595.

61   Groome-porter] Officer of the Lord Chamberlain, responsible for regulation of gaming.

119   *Sea-coale*-lane] Off Snow Hill near Fleet Street.

124   water-worke] Myddleton's New River scheme began in 1609 and was completed in 1613.

143  soveraigne etc.] A Henry VIII
sovereign was worth 10s., a groat
4d., a noble 6s. 8d.; the Mary
coins are perhaps preferred by the
fairies, traditionally "of the old
religion", as being minted in
Catholic times.

### III. V

31  DOL enters . . . ] Possibly the
S.D. in F is mistaken, and Dol
should play off-stage; "What
newes, DOL?" at l. 49 is a natural
entry.

### IV. I

56  Austriack] The heavy Hapsburg
lip was famous; the Valois nose
and the Medici forehead are J's
jokes.
90  KELLEY] Emperor Rudolf II
favoured Edward Kelley (1555–
1595), Dee's partner, in his gold-
making.
92  ÆSCULAPIUS] Legendary doctor
slain by Zeus's lightning, lest he
should overcome death entirely.
145  POPPÆA] Nero's mistress,
named here because her name
means "doll": J's joke, not
Mammon's, since he apparently
does not know her name.
156  free state] English law forbade
a private subject to practise alchemy without royal permission;
del Rio (ed. of 1657, p. 94) wished
that other countries had the same
law.

### IV. II

7  flap] Face longs for a suit that
could be put on instantly, so that
he could have his chance with Dame
Pliant immediately.

21  Grammar etc.] Subtle applies
the terminology of formal grammar, logic and rhetoric to duelling.

### IV. III

21  Sennores . . . ] "Gentlemen, I kiss
your hands".
29  D'ALVA] The Duke of Alva,
governor of the Netherlands 1567–
73, executed the Flemish patriot
Count Egmont in 1568.
34  Por dios . . . ] "Gad, gentlemen,
a very pretty house".
40  Entiendo] "I understand".
47  Con . . . ] "Please, may I see this
lady?".
61  Entiendo . . . ] "I understand, that
the lady is so beautiful, that I am
as anxious to see her, as for the
best fortune of my life".
78  Sennores . . . ] "Gentlemen, why
this delay?".
80  Puede . . . ] "Maybe you are
mocking my love".
91  Por . . . ] "By this honoured
beard".
92  Tiengo . . . ] "I fear, gentlemen,
you are practising some treachery
on me".

### IV. IV

3  Spanish] James I's pro-Spanish
policy, though politically un-
popular, encouraged a fashion for
all things Spanish.
32  rush] Picked up from the floor.
33  straw-berries . . . mackrell] She
will sink to hawking fruit and fish
in the streets.
47  Exchange etc.] Mentioned also in
Silent Woman I. III, IV. III, as
London sights. The New Exchange was opened in 1609;
Bethlehem Hospital (Bedlam), the

madhouse, was a standard attraction; China-houses were shops selling newly imported eastern goods.

53   *Que . . .* ] "How is it, sirs, that she does not come? This delay is killing me".

57   *Por tódos . . .* ] "By all the gods, the most perfect beauty I have seen in my life".

63   *El Sol . . .* ] "The sun has lost his light with the splendour this lady brings, so help me God!"

69   *Por que . . .* ] "Why does she not come to me?"

71   *Por el . . .* ] "For the love of God, why does she delay?"

76   *Sennora . . .* ] "My lady, my person is quite unworthy to approach such beauty".

80   *Sennora, si . . .* ] "Lady, if it is convenient, let us go in".

### IV. V

1-32   *For . . . Rome*] Dol is wickedly garbling the already garbled *Concent of Scripture* (c. 1590, the larger revised edition, S.T.C. 3851, no place or date given) by Broughton (see comment on II. III. 238), a wild chronology harmonising secular history with scriptural prophecy. The "legs" are those of a giant, symbolising the Hellenistic kingdoms crushing the Jews. The "chaine" is a chronological subdivision. Javan = Greek, Thogarma = Tigranes, habergions = coats of mail, Cittim = Italy, Abaddon and the Beast = the Pope, and "Helens" is somebody's blunder for "Hebers", = Hebrew.

26   fift *Monarchy*] The four beasts of *Daniel* VII and the four kingdoms of *Daniel* II were Assyria, Persia,

Greece and Rome; the fifth monarchy to be set up, according to contemporary enthusiasts, was that of Christ and his saints, as predicted in the Apocalypse.

### IV. VII

40   AMADIS *de Gaule*] Hero of 15th century popular romance of Spanish origin, of a type despised by J.

41   *cox-combe*] Surly's "leud hat" (l. 55); and probably, as Dr Gurr suggests to me, with a memory of *The Knight of the Burning Pestle*.

45   *Otter . . . Tim*] The exact sense of these abusive terms is obscure; "whit" perhaps = "particle", and "tim" = "small boy".

53   uncleane birds] Not D'Alva's soldiers (H.S.). Strange birds with feathers of "divers coloures" like "great Ruffes" were caught on the coast of Lincolnshire (in 1586), and interpreted by a pamphleteer as warning prodigies against sin. J. may have mistaken the date, or there may have been another visitation: see M. A. Shaaber (bibliography).

69   play the foole] Implies that the actor who played Drugger was the company's professional fool: *i.e.* Armin.

71   HIERONYMO] Hero of Kyd's *Spanish Tragedy*, and therefore both old and appropriate.

125   *Ratcliffe*] On the river at Stepney.

### V. I

6   *Pimlico*] Not the modern district, but a house in Hoxton (cf. V. II. 19) noted for its ale.

### v. ii

20  *Eye-bright*] Uncertain; a kind of ale, or the name of an inn or its keeper.

### v. iii

21  FACE] Surly does not recognise him; he means "insolence", "insolent creature". Perhaps F is wrong in printing in capitals, as for proper names.

### v. iv

10–15  I have . . . with it] The long parenthesis indicates that the conversation is out of Dapper's hearing.

41  *Wool-sack* etc.]. The Wool-sack was an inn in Faringdon Ward; for Dagger see comment on I. I. 191. "Heaven" and "Hell" were taverns on the site of the present House of Commons.

77  *Brainford*] Brentford, some 7 miles west of London.

89  *pigeons*] The Three Pigeons Inn at Brentford; cf. *She Stoops to Conquer*.

101  readie] As often, refers specifically to dress; here, the Spanish costume.

116  WARD] Notorious Mediterranean pirate. Daborne's play, *A Christian Turn'd Turke*, acted 1609, was based on his life.

129  I sent for him] Untrue; Face is still twisting.

141  AMO . . . *Cæsarean*] Presumably brothel-keepers; cf. Madame Caesar, *Epig.* cxxxiii.

### v. v

14  BEL] See *Apocrypha*, "Bel and the Dragon".

117  HARRY NICHOLAS] Henrick Niclaes, Anabaptist mystic, leader of the "family of love", and author of *Enterlude of Minds* (1574).

121  *Westchester*] Chester.

159  *decorum*] Fitness: a fundamental critical concept denoting artistic and moral coherence.

# BIBLIOGRAPHY

## ABBREVIATIONS

## I. JONSON'S WORKS

### A. GENERAL

*Workes.* *First Folio, 1616.

*Workes.* Second Folio, 1640.

*Ben Jonson*, edd. C. H. Herford, Percy and Evelyn Simpson. Oxford (Oxford U.P.) 1925–52.

### B. *THE ALCHEMIST*

*The Alchemist.* First Quarto, 1612.

*The Alchemist*, ed. H. C. Hart. London (De la More Press) 1903.

*The Alchemist*, ed. C. M. Hathaway, in *Yale Studies in English*, XVII New York (Yale U.P.) 1903.

*The Alchemist.* First Quarto, 1612, in the Noel Douglas Replicas series. London (Noel Douglas) 1927.

*The Alchemist*, ed. R. J. Kingsford. Cambridge (Cambridge U.P.) 1928 and 1965.

*The Alchemist*, ed. H. Spencer, in *Elizabethan Plays*. London (Macmillan) 1934.

*Ben Jonson's "The Alchemist"*, ed. H. de Vocht, in *Materials for the study of the Old English Drama*, XXII. Louvain (Librairie Universitaire) 1950.

*The Alchemist*, ed. J. I. McCollum jr. New York (Barron) 1965.

*The Alchemist*, ed. D. Brown. London (Benn) 1966.

## II. STUDIES OF JONSON

### A. GENERAL

#### 1. *Textual*

GERRITSEN, J. "Stansby and Jonson Produce a Folio. A Preliminary Account", in *E.S.*, XL (1959), pp. 52–5.

F

### 2. *Critical*

ARMSTRONG, W. A. "Ben Jonson and Jacobean Stagecraft", in *Stratford-upon-Avon Studies* I (1960), pp. 43–61.

BAMBOROUGH, J. B. *Ben Jonson*. London (Longmans) 1959.

BARISH, J. A. *Ben Jonson and the Language of Prose Comedy*. Cambridge (Harvard U.P.) 1960.

ELIOT, T. S. "Ben Jonson", in *Selected Essays*. London (Faber) 1958.

ENCK, J. J. *Jonson and the Comic Truth*. Madison, Wis. (Wisconsin U.P.) 1957.

GOODMAN, P. *The Structure of Literature*. Chicago (Chicago U.P.) 1954.

HAYS, H. R. "Satire and Identification: An Introduction to Ben Jonson", in *Kenyon Review*, XIX (1957), pp. 267–83.

JOHANSSON, B. *Religion and Superstition in the Plays of Ben Jonson and Thomas Middleton*. Upsala (Lundequist) 1950.

KERNAN, A. *The Cankered Muse*. New Haven (Yale U.P.) 1959.

KNIGHTS, L. C. *Drama and Society in the Age of Jonson*. London (Chatto & Windus) 1937.

LEVIN, H. Introduction to Nonesuch edition of *Selected Works*. New York (Random House) n.d. [1938].

NOYES, R. G. *Ben Jonson on the English Stage 1660–1776*. Cambridge (Harvard U.P.) 1935.

PARTRIDGE, E. B. *The Broken Compass*. London (Chatto & Windus) 1958.

PUTNEY, R. "Jonson's Poetic Comedy", in *P.Q.*, XLI (1962), pp. 188–204.

REDWINE, J. D. "Beyond Psychology: The Moral Basis of Jonson's Theory of Humour Characterization", in *E.L.H.*, XXVIII (1961), pp. 316–34.

SACKTON, A. H. *Rhetoric as a Dramatic Language in Ben Jonson*. New York (Columbia U.P.) 1948.

THAYER, C. G. *Ben Jonson, Studies in the Plays*. Oklahoma (Oklahoma U.P.) 1963.

TOWNSEND, F. L. *Apologie for Bartholomew Fayre*. London (Oxford U.P.) 1947.

### B. *THE ALCHEMIST*

#### 1. *Textual*

DAVIS, H. "Note on a Cancel in 'The Alchemist', 1612", in *The Library* (5th series), XIII (1958), pp. 278–90.

## 2. *Critical*

DUNCAN, E. H. "Jonson's *The Alchemist* and the Literature of Alchemy", in *P.M.L.A.*, LXI (1946), pp. 699–710.

KNOLL, R. E. "How to Read *The Alchemist*", in *College English*, XXI (1959–60) pp. 456–60.

McCULLEN, J. T. "Conference with the Queen of Fairies", in *S.N.*, XXIII (1950–1), pp. 87–95.

SHAABER, M. A. "The 'Uncleane Birdes' in *The Alchemist*", in *M.L.N.*, LXV (1950), pp. 106–9.

F*

# GLOSSARY

Usually only the first appearance of each meaning is given; the metaphorical or punning senses of alchemical terms are given only when not obvious. Puns are indicated by (*a*) . . . (*b*) . . . "Alch." = alchemical.

| | |
|---|---|
| adalantado | *provincial governor,* III. III. 50. |
| affections | *feelings,* DED. l. 5; *appetites,* II. VI. 17, *cf.* affects = *likes,* III. IV. 71. |
| alkaly | *soda-ash,* I. III. 76. (alch.) |
| aludel | *pear-shaped pot open at both ends,* II. III. 35. (alch.) |
| amalgama | *mixture of metal and mercury,* II. III. 79. (alch.) |
| amus'd | *puzzled,* I. III. 43. |
| andirons | *bars for burning wood,* II. III. 116. |
| anenst | *opposite,* II. VI. 22. |
| angel | *gold coin worth ten shillings,* I. II. 37. |
| antickes | *grotesque performer or performance,* EPIS. l. 6. |
| aqua regis | *acid solvent of gold,* II. V. 27. (alch.) |
| argaile | *cream of tartar,* I. III. 76. (alch.) |
| art, man of | *practitioner of secret skills,* IV. II. 48; *cf.* artist, IV. I. 82, filius artis, *son of art,* II. V. 8. (alch.) |
| ascension | *distillation, evaporation,* II. III. 98. (alch.) |
| assiduitie | *frequency,* DED. l. 10. |
| assumpsit | *undertaking entered into for some reward,* I. II. 69. |
| athanor | *digesting furnace,* II. III. 45. (alch.) |
| attorney, by | *disguised, in another person,* II. III. 297. |
| aurum potabile | *medicinal gold* (in context, = *bribe*), III. I. 41. (alch.) |
| balneum | *bath, of sand or water,* II. III. 41. (alch.) |
| barbel | *bearded carp,* II. II. 82. |
| bath, S. Maries | *bain Marie, water-bath,* II. III. 61. (alch.) |
| bird | *familiar spirit* (= fly), I. II. 87; *woman,* V. IV. 82; (verb) *prey,* or *nest,* V. V. 12. |
| bolt(s)-head | *globular flask with long neck,* II. II. 9., IV. V. 61. (alch.) |
| bona roba | *handsome wench* (properly, *well-dressed*), II. VI. 30. |
| botcher | *tailor who does repairs,* III. II. 113. |
| boy | *riotous youth,* III. III. 82. |
| brach | *bitch,* I. I. 111. |
| broke | *opened discussion,* I. II. 10. |
| bufo | *toad, base earth, terra,* II. V. 81. (alch.) |
| burgesses | *members of parliament* (probably), II. II. 62. |

calcination, calcine: *heating the substance, stage no.* 1, II. III. 63; the powder
remaining is "calx", II. III. 64, or "calce", II. V. 35. (alch.)

calverd *sliced while alive (probably),* II. II. 80.

canting *thieves' slang,* II. III. 42.

case *disguise,* IV. V. 103.

cast *cashiered,* III. IV. 76.

ceration *reduction to wax-like consistency,* II. V. 23. (alch.)

child *chylde, youth of gentle birth,* IV. IV. 38.

chrysopœia *gold-making,* II. V. 14. (alch.)

cibation *feeding, addition of new matter, stage no.* 7, I. I. 151. (alch.)

cinoper *cinnabar, crystalline mercuric sulphide,* I. III. 77. (alch.)

citronise *attain colour of completed digestion,* III. II. 129. (alch.)

cocatrice *monster, prostitute,* V. III. 34.

cohobation *re-distillation,* II. V. 23. (alch.)

collect *recollect,* I. I. 23.

colour *pretext,* III. III. 17; for alch. sense, see note on II. II. 25.

compeere *comrade,* III. III. 11.

concumhere *fornicate,* IV. I. 30.

congelation, congeal: *hardening by cold, stage no.* 6, II. III. 104. (alch.)

copie *copiousness,* EPIS. l. 30; *style,* V. V. 134.

coyle *tumult,* V. IV. 14.

crewell *(a) worsted yarn, (b) cruel,* I. I. 173.

crinckle *shrink, recoil,* III. V. 76.

crosse-let *crucible, melting pot,* I. III. 103. (alch.)

crow, crowes-head: *sign of black colour,* II. II. 26, II. III. 68. (alch.)

cucurbite *gourd-shaped vessel,* I. III. 103. (alch.)

cut *engraved (as of a picture),* I. I. 98; *(noun) chance in lottery,*
I. I. 178.

deceptio visus *optical illusion,* V. III. 62.

diameter, in *directly opposite, the lie direct,* III. IV. 39.

digestion *treating by gentle heat and moisture,* II. III. 73. (alch.)

dildo *phallus, perhaps with reference to a song,* V. V. 42.

discipline *ecclesiastical policy or party,* II. IV. 31; *military art,* III. III. 35.

discover *disclose,* I. II. 25.

distillation *chemistry, and more specifically the separation of volatile from
fixed parts,* IV. I. 84. (alch.)

dog-bolt *term of contempt of uncertain meaning,* I. I. 121.

donzel *young gentleman, squire,* IV. III. 39.

doome *judgment, sentence,* IV. III. 73.

downeward *indeed (?),* V. I. 41.

edified *profited spiritually,* III. I. 45.

emp'ricks *empyricks, experimenters, quacks,* IV. I. 136.

entrailes *linings,* II. I. 16.

ephemerides *astronomical almanacs,* IV. VI. 48.

epididimis *gland behind testicles,* III. III. 22.

| | |
|---|---|
| exaltation, exalt | *a purificatory process, sometimes equated with sublimation,* I. I. 68. (alch.) |
| exercises | *extempore effusions,* III. II. 54. |
| | |
| fæces | *sediment,* II. III. 63. (alch.) |
| fall | *flat band,* II. III. 306. |
| faithfull | *believing,* II. I. 29. |
| feature | *form, proportion,* IV. I. 75. |
| feize | *frighten, beat,* V. V. 131. |
| fermentation, ferment: | *process involving leaven, working by heat and effervescence,* I. I. 151. (alch.) |
| figs | *piles (probably),* I. I. 3. |
| figure | *horoscope,* I. I. 96; (a) *horoscope,* (b) *bosom,* IV. IV. 92. |
| firke | *move quickly or suddenly (transitively or intransitively)* II. I. 28, II. IV. 5. |
| fixation, fix | *stage when substance no longer flies from heat,* I. I. 68. (alch.) |
| flaw'd | *flayed,* IV. III. 100. |
| flitter-mouse | *bat,* V. IV. 88. |
| flower | *essence, also powder produced by sublimation,* II. I. 47. (alch.) |
| fly | *familiar spirit,* I. II. 43. |
| foyst | *pickpocket, rogue,* IV. VII. 16. |
| french beanes | *broad beans,* I. III. 29. |
| fricace | *rub,* III. II. 40. |
| friers | *Blackfriars,* I. I. 17. |
| frume(n)ty | *wheat boiled in milk and seasoned,* V. IV. 42. |
| fucus | *cosmetic wash,* I. III. 73. |
| furnus acediæ | *slow furnace,* III. II. 3. (alch.) |
| | |
| garbe | *fashion,* IV. IV. 10. |
| ging | *gang,* V. I. 21. |
| gleeke | *fashionable card game,* II. III. 285. |
| God make you rich: | *a kind of backgammon,* V. IV. 45. |
| gold-end-man | *one who buys scraps (ends) of gold,* II. IV. 21. |
| goldsmith | *usurer,* I. III. 32. |
| goose-turd | *yellow green,* IV. IV. 50. |
| graced | *in a position of power,* III. II. 56. |
| graines | *spices,* I. III. 25; *weight,* II. VI. 89; *corn,* III. III. 6. |
| gripes egge | *griffin's egg, an oval vessel,* II. III. 40. (alch.) |
| ground | *basic material, terra,* II. III. 67. (alch.) |
| guiny-bird | *prostitute,* IV. I. 38. |
| | |
| happinesse | *aptness,* IV. I. 23. |
| hargubuzier | *musketeer,* V. V. 56. |
| hay | *net stretched between rabbit-holes,* II. III. 71. |
| helme | *alembic, upper vessel used in sublimation,* II. I. 98. (alch.) |
| heterogene | *impure, of mixed substance,* II. V. 11. (alch.) |

hieroglyphick          *symbol*, II. VI. 24.
hoighs                 *hoys, sloop-rigged vessels*, III. III. 14.
homogene               *pure, of uniform substance*, II. V. 11. (alch.)
honest                 *chaste*, IV. V. 54, IV. VII. 103.
horses                 *lottery tickets*, I. I. 193.
house                  *ʒodiacal sign*, I. I. 96.
huishers               *ushers*, IV. IV. 45.

idiot                  *ignorant man*, II. III. 201.
i-fac                  *in faith* (presumably a coy euphemism), I. II. 129.
imbibition             *steeping in liquor*, II. III. 59. (alch.)
inceration             *reduction to wax-like consistency*, II. III. 84. (alch.)
instrument             *set of instructions*, II. VI. 69, III. IV. 28; *means*, III. I. 16;
                       *agreement*, V. IV. 81.

jealousie              *suspicion*, IV. I. 119.
jovy'                  *jovial*, V. V. 144.
junctura annularis     *joint of ring-finger*, IV. II. 47.
just                   *exactly*, I. III. 8.

Kastril                *kestrel*, passim.
kemia                  *distilling vessel* (?), II. III. 99. (alch.)
kibes                  *chilblains*, I. I. 35.
knot                   *kind of snipe*, II. II. 81.

lac Virginis           *virgin's milk, a synonym for the stone as liquid substance*,
                       II. III. 62. (alch.)
lembeke                *alembic*, III. II. 4. (alch.)
lent                   *slow, mild (of heat)* II. III. 45. (alch.)
liberties              *suburbs*, IV. VII. 116.
linea fortunæ          *line of fortune, from little finger to first finger*, IV. II. 45.
lotium                 *lye, made from urine*, IV. VII. 33.
lunarie                *synonym for the stone (also various plants)*, II. III. 283. (alch.)
lute, lutum            *seal with clay*, II. III. 40, 285. (alch.)

maistry                *magisterium* (see note on I. IV. 14), IV. I. 122; *masterpiece*
                       III. III. 8. (alch.)
mammet                 *puppet*, V. V. 128.
mark                   *silver worth* 13s. 4d. *by weight*, I. I. 56.
Mars                   *iron*, II. III. 75. (alch.)
mathematiques          *astrology*, IV. I. 83.
mauther                *awkward girl*, IV. VII. 23.
ṁeere                  *absolute*, V. III. 2.
menstrue, menstruum:   *solvent*, I. I. 116, II. III. 286. (alch.)
merds                  *ordure*, II. III. 195.
metaposcopie           (properly "metoposcopy"), *the art of telling fortunes and
                       character from the face*, I. III. 44.

| | |
|---|---|
| moderne | *commonplace*, IV. I. 23. |
| mons Veneris | *flesh at base of thumb, also in sexual sense*, IV. II. 46. |
| mortification | *destruction of active qualities of substance*, II. V. 25. (alch.) |
| motion | *puppet-show*, V. I. 22. |
| mum-chance | *a dice game*, V. IV. 44. |
| myrobalane | *plum or sweetmeat* (?), IV. II. 42. |
| | |
| naturalls | *native ability*, EPIS. l. 10. |
| naturiz'd | *naturata, created* (*nature*), II. I. 64. |
| nipp'd | *pinched together, of the neck of a flask*, II. III. 73. |
| numerous | *harmonious*, EPIS. l. 33. |
| nun | *prostitute*, V. V. 20. |
| | |
| ordinary | *eating house*, I. II. 100; ordinarily: (*a*) *commonly*, (*b*) *according to eating house custom*, III. IV. 40. |
| | |
| pamphysick | *universal*, II. V. 15 (perhaps coined by Jonson). |
| panarchick | *all-ruling, sovereign*, II. V. 15 (perhaps coined by Jonson). |
| parcell guilt | *partly gilded*, III. II. 45; parcell-broker, *part-time go-between*, IV. VI. 33. |
| partie-bawd | *partner in bawdry*, III. III. 11. |
| passe-time | *time-piece* (probably a verbal whimsy), I. II. 8. |
| pellicane | *vessel with down-curved neck, resembling the bird*, II. III. 78. (alch.) |
| pellitorie | *plant used as medicine*, III. IV. 120. |
| perspective | *optical instrument for viewing objects*, III. IV. 87. |
| philosopher, philosophicall: | *alchemist, alchemical*, I. I. 71, II. III. 264. (alch.) |
| phlegma | *phlegm, watery tasteless substance got by distillation*, II. V. 2. (alch.) |
| piger Henricus | *slow furnace* (*fauler Heintze*), II. V. 80. (alch.) |
| pin-dust | *fine metallic dust*, II. V. 71. |
| pistolets | *Spanish coin worth about £1*, III. III. 15. |
| plot | *ground-plan*, I. III. 9. |
| poesies (of candle): | *marks of candle-smoke*, V. V. 41. |
| portague | *Portuguese gold coin worth about £4*, I. III. 87. |
| posts, swift | *as swiftly as post-horses*, III. IV. 79. |
| presently | *immediately*, IV. VII. 17. |
| prevent | *anticipate*, II. III. 6. |
| prevaricate | *proceed crookedly*, II. III. 19. |
| primero | *fashionable card game*, II. III. 284. |
| project, projection: | *the final stage, no. 12, when a substance is transformed, by "throwing on" the tincture*, I. I. 79. (alch.) |
| puck-fist | *empty boaster*, I. II. 63. |
| punque | *whore*, II. I. 23; punque, device: *arrant whore*, (*cf.* "point-device"), V. III. 50; punquettees, *exact sense uncertain*, II. I. 23. |
| purchase | *winnings*, IV. VII. 122. |

putrefaction | *decomposition, when the substance falls to the bottom of the vessel,* II. V. 21. (alch.)

queene | (*a*) *of Faery,* (*b*) *quean, whore,* V. IV. 65.
quiblins | *tricks,* IV. VII. 110.
quodling | *raw apple or youth,* I. I. 189.

rage | *madness,* IV. I. 10.
reaching | *offering,* I. IV. 20.
receiver, recipient | *vessel for receiving the product of distillation,* IV. V. 61, II. V. 1. (alch.)
register | *sliding plate on furnace to control heat,* II. III. 33. (alch.)
reverberate | *to heat in a furnace where the flames are "beaten back" from the top,* II. III. 66. (alch.)
ride | *be carted as a whore,* I. I. 167.
rifle | *gamble, raffle,* I. I. 193.
riot | *debauchery, dissipation,* II. II. 92.
rivo frontis | *vein of forehead,* IV. II. 43.
ruby | *the stone in its red phase of perfection,* II. I. 48. (alch.)
rudenesse | *lack of art,* EPIS. l. 17.
rugg | *coarse cloth,* II. VI. 21; *felt of rugg, hat of such cloth,* I. I. 36.

sanguine | *sexy,* II. IV. 11.
sapiens | =*philosopher, q.v.;* II. III. 285. (alch.)
scheme | *horoscope,* IV. IV. 18.
seeme | *be seen,* I. III. 71.
sericon | *red tincture,* II. V. 81. (alch.)
sess'd | *assessed,* III. IV. 123.
set | *stake against,* I. II. 81; *fold of ruff,* IV. III. 33; *set out, raise (voice),* V. III. 67.
severall | *separated, divided up,* IV. II. 67.
shorten eares | *have ears cut off,* III. II. 87.
sicknesse | *plague,* ARG. l. 1.
sign'd with Hermes seale: *hermetically sealed (from Hermes Trismegistus),* II. III. 79. (alch.)
silver potate | *liquid silver,* III. II. 128. (alch.)
single money | *small change,* V. IV. 114.
slopps | *wide breeches or hose,* III. III. 13.
solæcisme | *incongruity,* IV. I. 101.
sordide | *mean, low,* EPIS. l. 23.
sort | *crowd,* I. I. 164.
sound | *sane,* I. I. 99; *healthy,* III. II. 39.
souse | *ears of pig,* IV. III. 27.
spagirica | *alchemy,* II. V. 14. (alch.)
spectatissimi | *especially looked up to,* II. I. 8.
spittle | *hospital,* I. IV. 23.

| | |
|---|---|
| spur-ryall | *noble of Edward IV, with a design like a spur,* III. V. 33. |
| start | *advantage,* III. II. 72. |
| statelich | *stately (German),* II. IV. 7. |
| state(s) | *estates, property,* III. III. 30; *rank, status,* III. V. 16. |
| stiles | *titles of honour,* IV. I. 118. |
| still | *constantly,* PROL., l. 10. |
| stoupe | *stoope, bow,* IV. IV. 10; *swoop, as of a hawk,* V. V. 135. |
| sublimination, sublime: | *heating of substances to make them rise,* I. I. 68. (alch.) |
| succubæ | *concubines,* II. II. 48. |
| sufficient | *capable,* EPIS. l. 13; *financially sound* III. IV. 89. |
| | |
| table dormant | *permanent side table,* V. V. 103. |
| taile | *(a) entail, (b) female sexual organs,* II. VI. 87. |
| taw'd | *suppled, softened up,* IV. III. 100. |
| teaching i'the nose: | *preaching with puritan intonation,* V. I. 11. |
| terra damnata | *base earth remaining in vessel,* II. V. 5. (alch.) |
| terrae filius | *(a) landed proprietor, (b) rustic,* IV. II. 13. |
| threaves | *droves,* V. II. 19. |
| tincture, tinct | *a substance capable of transforming another to its own nature or colour, but used loosely,* I. I. 76. (alch.) |
| tit | *young girl,* V. V. 80. |
| titillation | *method of perfuming gloves,* IV. IV. 13. |
| tom-boy | *young girl,* V. V. 80. |
| tray-trip | *dice game depending on throwing threes (trey),* V. IV. 44. |
| trig | *coxcomb,* IV. VII. 39. |
| trunkes | *padded breeches, trunk hose,* III. III. 14. |
| turris circulatorius: | *vessels mounted one on another for circulating liquids,* III. II. 3. (alch.) |
| tyre | *woman's head-dress,* III. III. 78. |
| | |
| upsee Dutch | *Dutch fashion, phlegmatic,* IV. VI. 23. |
| | |
| vegetall | *vegetable,* I. I. 39; (?) *active, healthy, =vegetus,* II. III. 256 |
| vented | *spent,* III. IV. 52. |
| Venus | *copper,* II. I. 39. (alch.) |
| verdugo-ship | *mock title, verdugo=hangman,* III. III. 71. |
| vertuall | *powerful,* II. VI. 17; (*cf.* vertue=*skill,* IV. V. 110). |
| vicar | *vicar-general, bishop's deputy,* I. II. 50. |
| vile | *of little worth,* EPIS. l. 24. |
| vivification | *restoration of active qualities of a substance,* II. V. 25. (alch.) |
| | |
| water | *love-philtre* (?), II. VI. 55. |
| wood | *crowd* (=*silva*), III. II. 95. |
| wriggled | *slashed, intricately carved,* IV. III. 27. |